[redacted]

The Pharmacy Professional's Guide to Résumés, CVs, & Interviewing

[redacted]

The Pharmacy Professional's Guide to Résumés, CVs, & Interviewing

4th Edition

Thomas P. Reinders

APhA
PUBLICATIONS
Washington, DC

Managing Editor: Linda L. Young
Acquiring Editors: Julian I. Graubart, Janan Sarwar
Editorial Services: Linda L. Young, Potomac Indexing, LLC
Design and Layout: Circle Graphics
Cover Design: Scott Neitzke, APhA Creative Services

APhA was founded in 1852 as the American Pharmaceutical Association.

Published by the American Pharmacists Association
2215 Constitution Avenue, NW
Washington, DC 20037
www.pharmacist.com www.pharmacylibrary.com

To comment on this book via e-mail, send your message to the publisher at aphabooks@aphanet.org.

Library of Congress Cataloging-in-Publication Data

Names: Reinders, Thomas P., author. | American Pharmacists Association, issuing body.
Title: The pharmacy professional's guide to résumés, CVs, & interviewing / Thomas P. Reinders.
Description: Fourth edition. | Washington, DC : American Pharmacists Association, [2017] | Includes bibliographical references and index.
Identifiers: LCCN 2017028961 | ISBN 9781582122687 (alk. paper)
Subjects: | MESH: Job Application | Pharmacists | Interviews as Topic | Vocational Guidance
Classification: LCC RS122.5 | NLM QV 21 | DDC 615/.1023--dc23 LC record available at https://lccn.loc.gov/2017028961

To Drs. Gloria and Don Francke, my early mentors,

for their guidance in planning and preparing my career in pharmacy.

And to my family for their continuing support

of my professional pursuits.

Contents

Preface

During my career as a pharmacy educator and employer, I analyzed hundreds of résumés and curricula vitae and conducted even more interviews. I noted that many people who were seeking pharmacy positions came across as competent and knowledgeable, but they did not devote the attention they should have to their written communication and interviewing skills. This oversight detracted from the positive impression they otherwise would have made. My mission in this book is to help people in all facets of the profession, from technicians and new graduates to veteran pharmacists, land interviews and then carry them off with aplomb.

The Pharmacy Professional's Guide to Résumés, CVs, & Interviewing is about creating a favorable impression on employers, admission committees, and selection panels. It offers insights for preparing powerful résumés, curricula vitae, personal statements, and cover letters; coaches you how to appear professional in interviews; and helps you formulate effective answers to frequently asked interview questions. Although many publications and career coaches offer similar guidance, this book's unique focus is pharmacy professionals—those entering the profession, seeking an initial position, changing positions, choosing new directions, or returning to the profession after a hiatus.

Pulling together straightforward advice for pharmacists about the "perfect" résumé, CV, letter, or interview questions is challenging, because each segment of the profession has its own opinions and biases. Consequently, this book—based on my own experience as well as countless conversations with employers and applicants—should be seen as a resource to help you shape the approach that is right for you. It is not definitive and the sample documents included should not be viewed as templates.

This edition includes additional information about planning a career; creating a personal career map, personal statements, and letters of intent; using electronic portfolios to demonstrate accomplishments in skills and knowledge; using social media for personal branding; and presenting a professional image. Three animated videos have been created as supplements.

Be sure to seek input from colleagues, peers, and mentors throughout your job-seeking process. Their assistance, together with the wisdom of this book, should put you well on your way to obtaining your ideal pharmacy career position.

Thomas P. Reinders

Assessing Your Career Goals

CHAPTER 1

Contrary to what you might think, developing your résumé is not the first step in searching for a job. Before you even put pen to paper, you need to carefully assess your goals, strengths, values, and preferences to gain a clear perspective on where you stand now and where you want to go in the future. Unfortunately, many people put more thought into planning their next vacation than into mapping out their career. Whether you are a pharmacy technician seeking to become a pharmacist, a recent graduate seeking an entry-level pharmacist position, or a seasoned pharmacist looking for a new challenge, it pays to think through your goals—and then prepare a résumé designed to help you realize them.

The Career Pathway Evaluation Program

You may believe it is easy to select a career option in the pharmacy profession. But if you do a little research, you will find that the career possibilities go far beyond the traditional areas of community pharmacy or hospital practice. Table 1.1, taken from the *APhA Career Pathway Evaluation Program for Pharmacy Professionals*,[1] lists the many directions that pharmacy professionals can follow.

The APhA career pathway evaluation program, which includes exercises and a workbook, identifies many different career options, ranging from academia to regulatory affairs.[1] Pharmacy schools use this program to help students make informed career decisions. Individual pharmacists who are investigating new options find it helpful, too.

The APhA Career Pathway Evaluation Program for Pharmacy Professionals is designed to help you identify the appropriate pharmacy career option for you. To access the program, go to http://www.pharmacist.com/apha-career-pathway-evaluation-program-pharmacy-professionals.

Critical Job Factors

For each career option, the career pathway evaluation program details 48 critical job factors that you can use to evaluate which paths best suit you (Table 1.2). These factors represent six distinct areas: (1) future innovation and job fulfillment, (2) translation of knowledge to pharmacy practice, (3) relational, (4) workload, (5) non-salary compensation, and (6) freedom.

Reviewing these factors will give you an idea of how much patient counseling, professional interaction, problem solving, multitasking, innovative thinking, application of scientific or medical knowledge, and management of a business are involved in each career path. The summaries also cover such matters as work schedule, the amount of pressure involved, job security, prestige, income, and opportunities for advancement.

You should think about all these things carefully as you look at potential career choices. Many excellent books, workshops, and career counseling centers can also help you. Start by checking the internet or calling your local community college or a nearby university to find out about career development workshops.

Self-Assessment Survey Tool

The career pathway evaluation program has a convenient self-assessment survey tool that takes just 20 to 30 minutes to complete. Upon completion of the survey, you will receive a list of your possible career matches: each match will have a score that is based on an assessment of all 48 critical factors. A second set of scores will outline which critical factors you consider most important. Each score links to a specific pharmacy career profile that contains a background description of the position, an insider's perspective about what aspects of the position they find most and least appealing, and a brief commentary about how pharmacists in this career option rated each of the individual critical factors.

TABLE 1.1 Career Options for Pharmacy Professionals

COMMUNITY

Chain
Apothecary
Clinical*
Consultation
Franchise
Home health care
Long-term care
Medical group affiliate

Health Management Organization
Clinical*

Independent
Clinical*
Community health center
Compounding specialist
Consultation
Franchise
Home health care
Long-term care
Medical group affiliate
Office-based practice
Specialty services

INSTITUTION

Hospital (University, Community, Government)
Administration
Ambulatory care
Clinical*
Distribution and control
Investigational drugs
Long-term care
Medication use safety
Nuclear
Veterinary

CONSULTING
Clinical*
Consumer
Home health care
Long-term care
Managed care
Management/resource evaluation
Medicare/Medicaid
The Joint Commission

REGULATORY

State
Board of pharmacy
Consumer affairs
Department of health
Legislature
Medicare/Medicaid

Federal
Alcohol and drug abuse
Armed services
Centers for Medicare and Medicaid
Congress
Drug Enforcement Agency
Department of Health and Human Services
Food and Drug Administration
Health Care Financing Administration
Indian Health Service
Mental health
Public Health Service
Veterans Administration

INDUSTRY

Administration
Professional relations

Business
Management

Marketing
Sales

Research and Development
Administration
Basic research
Biological sciences
Clinical research
Medicinal chemistry
Pharmaceuticals
Pharmacognosy

Technical/Scientific
Drug information
Manufacturing
Medical affairs/medical liaison
Post-marketing surveillance
Product quality control
Regulatory affairs

ACADEMIA
Administration
Biological sciences
Clinical*
Continuing education
Experiential education
Medicinal chemistry
Pharmaceutics
Pharmacoeconomics
Pharmacognosy
Pharmacology
Pharmacotherapy
Pharmacy administration
Pharmacy practice

OTHER
Association management
Automation technology
Computer technology
Contract research organization
Mail service
Public policy and law
Publishing and communications
Third-party insurance
United States Pharmacopeia
Wholesaler

***Clinical**
Ambulatory care
Cardiology
Critical care
Dermatology
Drug information
Emergency medicine
Endocrinology
Gastroenterology
Geriatrics
Hematology
Immunology
Infectious diseases
Informatics
Internal medicine
Intravenous therapy
Nephrology
Neurology
Nutrition
Oncology
Pain management
Pediatrics
Pharmacogenomics
Pharmacokinetics
Poison control
Psychiatry
Rheumatology
Substance abuse
Surgery
Toxicology
Transplantation

*Adapted from reference 1.

TABLE 1.2 Critical Factors for Pharmacists' Practice Profiles

1. Interacting with patients
2. Conducting physical assessments
3. Interpreting laboratory values
4. Developing continuity of relationships
5. Helping people
6. Collaborating with other health professionals
7. Educating other professionals
8. Having variety in daily activities
9. Handling multiple tasks
10. Solving problems
11. Focusing on area of expertise
12. Thinking innovatively
13. Applying scientific knowledge
14. Applying medical knowledge
15. Creating new knowledge by conducting research
16. Managing/supervising others
17. Managing/supervising a business
18. Handling pressure/stress
19. Having acceptable work schedule
20. Having part-time opportunities
21. Having job-sharing opportunities
22. Having exit/re-entry opportunities
23. Having parental leave opportunities
24. Having leisure/family time
25. Having job security
26. Having opportunities for advancement
27. Having opportunities for leadership development
28. Having community prestige
29. Having professional involvement
30. Receiving good income
31. Receiving benefits (vacation, health, retirement)
32. Being in preferred geographic location
33. Having autonomy
34. Achieving a feeling of self-worth
35. Focusing on future
36. Receiving professional prestige
37. Receiving unique practice environment
38. Achieving advanced degree
39. Offering entrepreneurial opportunity
40. Offering additional training
41. Interacting with colleagues
42. Having opportunities to travel
43. Having opportunities to write
44. Working with a team
45. Being "on call"
46. Working on holidays
47. Working on weekends
48. Giving presentations

Source: Schommer JC, Brown LM, Sogol EM. *APhA Career Pathway Evaluation Program 2007 Pharmacist Profile Survey.* Washington, DC: American Pharmacists Association; June 2007.

The program offers additional insight about career planning through a series of interactive group exercises. You can also complete the exercises on your own to enhance your planning process. Some of the components include an assessment of your knowledge of career choices, your decision-making style, and an assignment of weights and values to each of the critical factors. The latter process allows you to complete a decision matrix that provides a reasonable basis for comparing career options.

The time spent to complete the survey and explore the exercises will benefit anyone interested in a career in pharmacy. For prospective students or pharmacy technicians, the program will provide a thorough overview of career options as well as information about whether their personal strengths match those outlined for pharmacists in a variety of practice settings. For pharmacy students and new graduates, the program offers an opportunity to assess which career options best suit their personal interests and strengths. Also, it will help detect areas that need strengthening with postgraduate study or training experiences. For practicing pharmacists, the program allows them to prioritize their professional needs and correlate them with practice areas that will most likely satisfy those needs. Achieving this goal may require a change in practice settings or even additional education and training.

Thinking Globally

Despite the practice setting, the health care employee marketplace has changed so markedly in the past decade that pharmacists must meet entirely new expectations. In her book *Career Intelligence,* Barbara Moses lists 12 rules to follow to achieve career success in today's world (see sidebar "Twelve Rules for Career Success" on next page). Successful workers in the "new economy"—an environment characterized by technology, information, and reengineering—think globally, remain sensitive to diverse cultures, and have powerful communication skills.

Identifying Your Personal Strengths

From an early age, individuals tend to focus on their weaknesses as a means of improving. However, focusing on faults does not always improve performance. Research conducted by the Gallup organization[2] has shown that you will achieve greater success by developing your strengths and leveraging your natural skills than you will by concentrating on your weaknesses. Also, understanding your strengths and enhancing them can help you strengthen your weaknesses.

Twelve Rules for Career Success

1. Ensure your marketability by building effective networks of colleagues.
2. Think globally. Today, geographic borders have disappeared and the entire world represents a potential market. Your ability to interact comfortably with other cultures will give you a distinct advantage.
3. Develop effective communication skills so you can convey your message in powerful and persuasive ways. These skills include conventional communication approaches, such as graphics, and the internet.
4. Commit yourself to lifelong learning. Employers like applicants who take personal responsibility for learning, both within and outside the work environment.
5. Understand business trends, including economic, demographic, and cultural factors, that impact the profession.
6. Prepare for areas of operational and clinical competence, rather than merely focusing on routine tasks and duties. You must develop skill sets and knowledge systems that you can transfer to a variety of different settings.
7. Seek to understand the profession's future by monitoring demographic, economic, and cultural trends.
8. Manage career effectiveness by building financial independence and soundly handling personal finances.
9. Discard the traditional notion of "career ladders" and envision a lattice instead, because you may need to move laterally to achieve upward mobility.
10. When deciding whether to pursue specialization or to follow the path of a generalist, conduct an objective assessment of your personal goals. For example, do you want to focus on technical aspects of the profession? Are you interested in clinical research? Do you hope to expand your credentials?
11. Learn to manage your time effectively, and know your priorities and limitations.
12. Take note of your successes and avoid dwelling on your mistakes or shortcomings. Instead, document your achievements so that you have a record of the many things you do well.

Source: Adapted from Moses B. *Career Intelligence*. San Francisco: Barrett-Koehler Publishers; 1998.

The Gallup organization[2] has developed an assessment tool to identify your strengths: *StrengthsFinder 2.0* measures 34 individual strengths (e.g., achiever, adaptability, competition, deliberativeness, futuristic, learner, responsibility, strategic) to prepare an individualized profile. The tool describes each strength and provides ideas for taking action and working with others who have the same strengths. The online tool summarizes your top five strengths, along with a host of strategies for applying these strengths in your personal life and professional activities.

Still another approach in helping to identify your personal strengths and talents is to select the top 10 adjectives that describe your personality and then compare them with a list of the top 10 adjectives selected by colleagues who know you. This exercise developed by Andrusia and Haskins[3] can be helpful in understanding how your self-image compares with how others see you (Table 1.3). In brief, learning about yourself is important for developing your career objective. This information will also be useful when you are planning for an interview session with a prospective employer who will seek information about your strengths and weaknesses.

Developing a Career Objective

Identifying a specific area of interest within the pharmacy profession will help you communicate to others exactly what you want and will enhance your chances of obtaining your desired position. You can state this area of interest at the beginning of a résumé or curriculum vitae (CV) in the form of a "career objective." Because a career objective is a long-range plan,

TABLE 1.3 Adjectives That Can Be Used to Create an Identity

Active	Helpful
Adaptable	Humorous
Ambitious	Imaginative
Assertive	Intelligent
Calm	Inventive
Candid	Leader-like
Cheerful	Likable
Competitive	Open-minded
Confident	Optimistic
Conservative	Orderly
Convincing	Organized
Cooperative	Original
Creative	Patient
Credible	Persuasive
Dependable	Productive
Diplomatic	Professional
Dynamic	Reliable
Easygoing	Resilient
Empowering	Resourceful
Encouraging	Savvy
Enterprising	Sensitive
Entertaining	Supportive
Enthusiastic	Tolerant
Ethical	Trusting
Experienced	Visionary
Extroverted	Well-adjusted
Flexible	Well-connected
Forward-thinking	Witty
Friendly	

Source: Adapted from Andrusia D, Haskins R. *Brand Yourself.* New York: Ballantine Books; 2000. Used with permission.

consider using only the term "objective" when your wording in this section is linked specifically to the position you wish to fill.

Pinpoint Your Objective

To pinpoint your objective, systematically assess your strengths, abilities, knowledge, skills, interests, and values. You also need to evaluate career options to identify possible matches for you. You might include one of the following career alternatives in your objective:

- To obtain a pharmacy technician position
- To obtain a pharmacy intern position
- To obtain a pharmacy practice residency position
- To obtain a pharmacy fellowship position
- To obtain a pharmacist position
- To obtain a pharmacy management position
- To obtain a clinical pharmacist position
- To join a health-system pharmacy where I can apply my knowledge and skills as a drug information specialist
- To obtain a tenure-eligible faculty position in pharmaceutics

Be Clear, Be Succinct

Narrow your choices to the objective that best suits you; then communicate it clearly and succinctly. Including your objective in your résumé or CV is considered optional, but expressing it with clarity—even if only for yourself—will help you identify the results you are seeking from your job search. The Sample Objectives box includes selected career objectives for someone seeking a pharmacy-related position.

References

1. *APhA Career Pathway Evaluation Program for Pharmacy Professionals*. Washington, DC: American Pharmacists Association; 2013.
2. Rath T. *StrengthsFinder 2.0.* New York: Gallup Press; 2007.
3. Andrusia D, Haskins R. *Brand Yourself.* New York: Ballantine Books; 2000.

CHAPTER 2

Planning Your Career Path

At every stage of your pharmacy career, you should assess your career goals and determine whether your current career path is allowing you to achieve what you want. Successful professionals make a commitment to lifelong learning. The pharmacy profession is no exception. To ensure success as a pharmacist, you will need to enhance your knowledge and skills to progress throughout your career.

Early Career Considerations

While you are a student pharmacist, actively explore pharmacy career options before you make a final career choice decision. The large number of practice site options, including community pharmacies, super markets, corporate chains, mass merchandisers, mail order pharmacies, specialty pharmacies, hospitals, long-term care facilities, managed care, and federal pharmacies, can be overwhelming. Your premature preference for one type of practice without evaluating other options can lead to missed opportunities and potential frustration later in your career as a practicing pharmacist.

Take full advantage of the educational opportunities provided through your exposure to practitioners during introductory and advanced pharmacy practice experiences. Join student pharmacist organizations to learn more about career options. Seek internship experience, even if your state does not require internship hours for licensure at the time of graduation. This sustained practice experience provides a solid foundation for pharmacy practice basics.

Faculty and pharmacists who practice in specialized settings often advise student pharmacists to pursue pharmacy residencies, fellowships, or graduate education after completing their professional degree. A pharmacy residency or fellowship will increase your knowledge and skills by providing opportunities to which other pharmacists may not be exposed. This type of accelerated training also provides additional knowledge and skills that otherwise would take several years to achieve. A graduate degree provides advanced knowledge and skills that are not usually available in residencies and fellowships. Degrees such as the Master of Science in the Pharmaceutical Sciences, Doctor of Philosophy in the Pharmaceutical Sciences, Master of Business Administration, Master of Public Health, and Master of Health Administration often are pursued by student pharmacists upon completion of their professional degree, or in combination with their professional degree if their school or college of pharmacy offers that option. Always weigh the advice of experienced and well-intentioned individuals against your personal circumstances before determining the right career path for yourself. Also, it is important to remember that you can enhance your knowledge and skills as a practitioner through alternative paths, such as part-time academic programs and certificate programs, and by gaining a variety of experience in different practice settings.

Mid-Career Considerations

With the wide variety of career options available, it is common for pharmacists to consider a career change. Additional reasons vary from employment termination to reentering the workforce after raising a family. Regardless of your reason for seeking change, you will need to honestly appraise your personal and professional assets before you start to search for a new position. No matter what stage of life you have reached, it is worthwhile to step back and ask yourself: Am I achieving what I want? Does my job contribute to, or detract from, my happiness? Am I comfortable with my career path, or do I want to change career directions? Do I need to develop new skills? Am I doing all I can to maintain and strengthen my knowledge?

In some cases, you may need to obtain additional education. If you have been working in one practice area and decide to transition to another practice area, then you may pursue self-study combined with selected continuing pharmacy education programs. You may consider the possibility of shadowing a colleague employed in the practice area you intend to pursue. You may determine that the education and skill set for the type of clinical practice you seek will require a structured education or training program. If you hold a

Doctor of Pharmacy degree, you may want to consider applying for a pharmacy residency, even though most of the applicants to those programs are recent graduates. If you do not hold this degree, you may consider enrolling in a nontraditional professional degree program. A few schools and colleges of pharmacy continue to offer this program, which can be ideal for the nontraditional student. A valuable information source about pharmacy residencies is available in the book *Getting Started in a Pharmacy Residency.*[1]

Another option is to seek certification from the Board of Pharmaceutical Specialties. At present there are eight recognized specialties: ambulatory care pharmacy, critical care pharmacy, nuclear pharmacy, nutrition support pharmacy, oncology pharmacy, pediatric pharmacy, pharmacotherapy, and psychiatric pharmacy. Each specialty has a corresponding certification examination that is administered twice annually. To ensure that knowledge and skills are maintained at the specialty level, pharmacists must recertify every 7 years. In addition, professional organizations such as the American Pharmacists Association and the National Association of Chain Drug Stores offer certification programs for practicing pharmacists.

Yet another option is to consider pursuing a graduate degree that will enhance your opportunities in the area of practice you intend to pursue. For example, if you are interested in a management position in a health-system practice, you might consider several degree options, including a Master of Health Administration (MHA), Master of Public Health (MPH), or Master of Business Administration (MBA). Your personal assessment of a specific program's content coupled with discussion of the program's strengths with graduates and their employers will assist you in determining an appropriate selection. Keep in mind that many pharmacists pursue graduate degrees on a part-time basis, often with financial assistance from their employer.

If you have been away from the workforce for several years, you may want to seek a more structured refresher course before seeking a position. Various state and national pharmacy associations offer a home study course that includes information about new drug entities, new medical therapies affected by drug usage, new employment conditions, new patient care services, computerization, demands of third-party payers, and new state and federal regulations. By participating in a refresher course, you can improve your knowledge and skills and enhance your confidence in returning to practice or changing your pharmacy career path.

Networking

Networking is a highly recommended method to ensure a successful outcome when you are planning to advance your career or change your career path. It is a process based on mutually beneficial relationships developed over time. This network will become important for discussing career options, seeking advice about changing your career path, seeking a new position, or serving as a reference. Your pharmacy colleagues, including classmates, employers, coworkers, and faculty, will likely serve as the initial source for preparing networking contacts, although other health professionals, family members, and friends should not be excluded. As a student pharmacist, you likely established a mentor relationship with several pharmacists and faculty members. Often these individuals will continue to be an invaluable source of support and encouragement throughout your career.

Making the most of your membership in professional organizations is an effective way to enhance your professional network. Becoming an active member of local, state, and national professional organizations will allow you to learn more about the opportunities within the profession and to enhance your professional network by meeting other pharmacists. Volunteering to serve and fulfilling leadership roles will significantly increase your professional networking opportunities.

Social media has become another channel for maintaining your network of professional colleagues and friends. Facebook and LinkedIn are two widely used electronic networking websites that provide opportunities to maintain connections with colleagues. Although Facebook is usually associated with social networking, student pharmacists and pharmacists rely on this website to maintain contact with colleagues, membership organizations, and their alma mater. LinkedIn is characterized as a business network website, and many users tend to be affiliated with corporations, although the presence of pharmacists, pharmacy organizations and schools, and colleges of pharmacy is increasing. At a minimum, this website provides an organized file of network contacts, including e-mail addresses. The profile feature serves as an effective networking process by allowing you to enter information readily available from your résumé and share it with other LinkedIn users. As a user, you can limit your account to the types of notifications you want to receive and the degree of information you want to share with other users. Additional information about the use of social media is included in Chapter 8.

Developing a Search Strategy for Changing Your Career Path

When searching for a position, you first need to identify potential employers. Many strategies exist—such as using the services of professional recruiters, reviewing advertisements in newspapers or professional journals, or looking at electronic listings of positions on the World Wide Web—but

FIGURE 2.1 Sample career map for a student pharmacist.

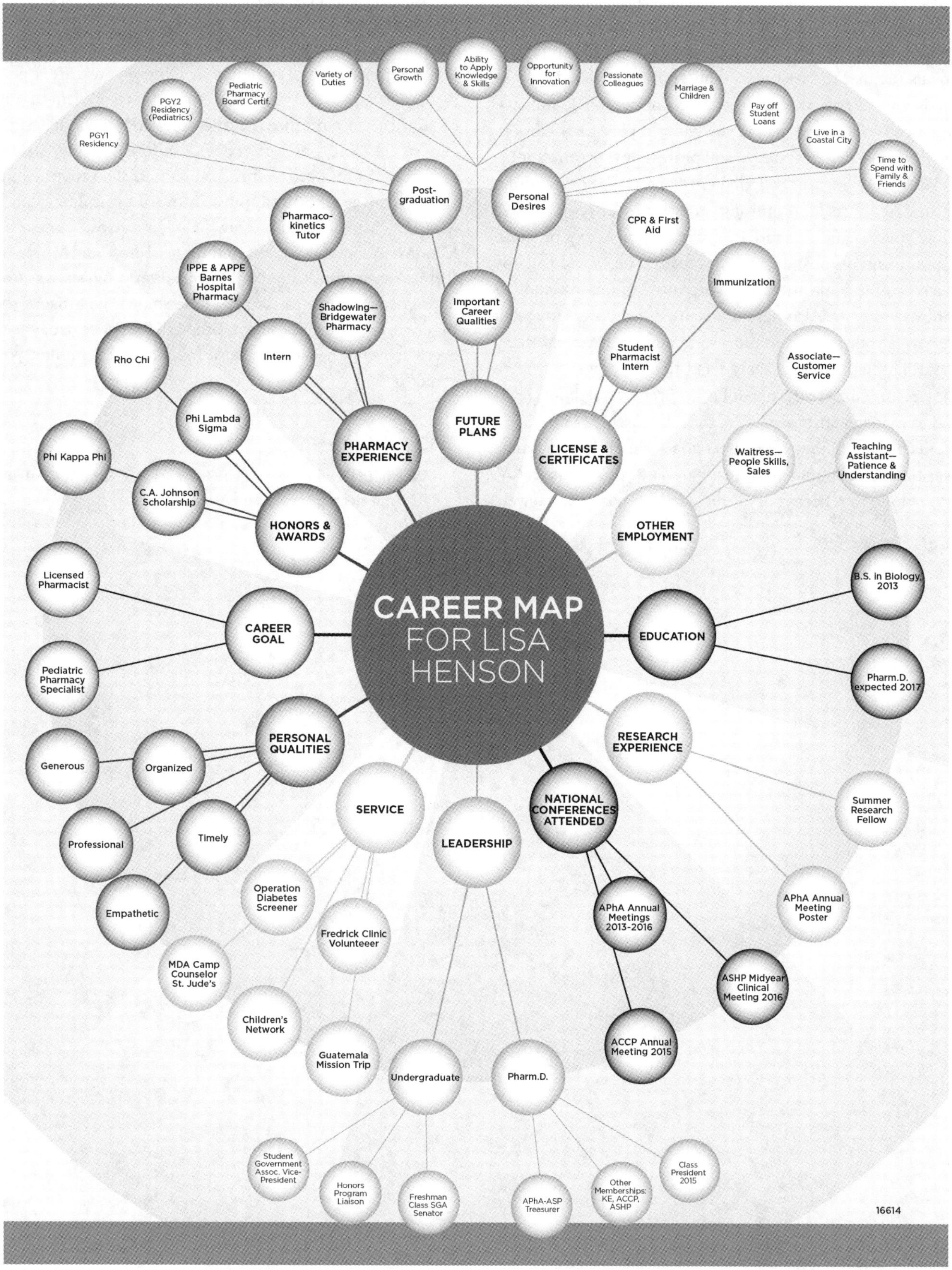

these strategies are not always successful. Within the pharmacy community, networking brings the most fruitful results for pinpointing key opportunities. In fact, most health professionals say that the best way to find positions suited to your needs and talents is to avail yourself of personal contacts: peers; coworkers; and people you know at pharmacy schools, corporations, health systems, and professional organizations.

Keep your résumé, curriculum vitae (CV), or portfolio up to date in case a promising opportunity arises. This will allow you to quickly send a copy in response to a position announcement, post a copy on websites, or provide a copy to a recruiter while attending a recruitment fair at a state or national meeting. Also, submit a well-crafted cover letter that expresses your interest in the position and requests an interview. The chapters that follow detail effective ways to prepare your résumé, CV, and portfolio; to prepare for interviews; and to manage other aspects of the job search.

Keep in mind that your career goals will probably change over time. You should continually update your résumé, CV, or portfolio to reflect your current situation. If your answers to the mid-career considerations lead you to seek new opportunities, having a current résumé, CV, or portfolio offers a big advantage.

An important tool to help you achieve your career goals is a personal career map. This tool creates a visual image of your career path that includes needed knowledge, skills, experience, and personal considerations such as character strengths and life events. You can create a map using a variety of free mind-mapping software programs such as Mind42 (https://mind42.com), Coggle (https://coggle.it/), MindMeister (https://www.mindmeister.com/), and MindMup (https://www.mindmup.com/). The latter program was used to prepare a sample career map for a student pharmacist (see Figure 2.1 on previous page). Although the process may seem overwhelming, it can be useful in visually examining your career path.

Reference

1. Miller ML. *Getting Started in a Pharmacy Residency.* Washington, DC: American Pharmacists Association; 2013.

Preparing Your Personal Statement and Letter of Intent

CHAPTER 3

Academic programs, residency and fellowship programs, and some employers may require more information about an applicant than a résumé, curriculum vitae (CV), or application form usually provides. Often a personal statement or letter of intent is requested. The two documents are different, but the terms often are used interchangeably, causing confusion. Before starting to prepare a draft document for this type of request, check whether the requestor can provide specific instructions or guidelines.

For either document, you will need to prepare a well-written statement that conveys your interest and potential for meeting the expectations of the program or employer. You will need to review your career plan and correlate your academic preparation and experiences with any stated requirements. Learn as much as possible about the program or employer by reviewing available electronic and print materials and speaking with colleagues who have personal knowledge. Based on your perceived needs of the program or employer, you will need to identify your pertinent experiences to include in your statement. In the absence of information about a character, word, or page limit, restrict either document to one page and do not exceed two pages.

Personal Statement

A personal statement offers evidence of your achievements and how they have shaped your knowledge, skills, and attitude. A major emphasis is to describe your passion for the type of program or employment you are seeking and why the particular program is a good fit for you. The reader should have a sense of who you are beyond the routinely requested information, such as reference letters and college transcripts. The statement should reflect why you are seeking the position, and it should be based on your personal experiences (e.g., education, professional practice, research, leadership, public service). Most often your personal statement will be structured in a chronological fashion, usually around a personal story or event that led you to pursue a particular program or employer. The document should consist of three to four paragraphs prepared in an essay format.

To help you prepare the statement, the requestor may supply an open-ended question such as "What led you to choose a career in pharmacy?" or "How will this program help you reach your professional goals?" However, in most cases you will need to develop your own statement. A theme is often developed in the form of a story. You can prepare your story using the STAR technique, which is often used for behavioral interviewing (see sidebar "STAR Technique" on next page). You may choose to use one or two of the following examples of themes:

- Address features of the position or program that are unique and most appealing to you.
- Discuss your personal, family, or friend's illness that led to your interest in becoming a health professional.
- Provide reflection about the inspiration you have acquired from a family member or mentor.
- Discuss employment and/or educational experiences that have shaped your motivation and ambitions.
- Discuss personal situations in which your problem-solving skills were effective.
- Provide reflection on hardships you have overcome and how the experience has strengthened your personal characteristics, such as empathy or persistence.
- Discuss your interest in and personal satisfaction associated with patient care.
- Discuss your career goals.
- Describe your personal attributes and how they will ensure future success in the position or program.

It is important to take the time to prepare a personal statement that is focused and well thought out, but do not let the task become a source of procrastination. Consider revealing enough information about yourself so that the reader relates to you and wants to get to know you better. Give examples or anecdotes that support your points. A brief story that

STAR Technique

S = Describe a SITUATION using enough background information to create a link to your role.

T = Outline an overview of the TASKS involved.

A = Describe the specific ACTIONS you took, either as an individual or a team member.

R = Summarize the RESULTS you achieved.

shows your positive attributes is more powerful than merely listing them. Definitely keep the statement's tone positive, and avoid recounting information in your résumé, CV, or portfolio. The personal statement in Figure 3.1 outlines the applicant's first and continued interest in community pharmacy practice.

Letter of Intent

A letter of intent is a statement of intention that serves as a nonbinding proposal to a program, institution, or employer. The letter serves to introduce you; your interest in being considered for a position; and a description of your applicable knowledge, skills, and attitude. A letter of intent can be viewed as a marketing document that is more focused than a personal statement and that is more of an extension of your résumé, CV, or portfolio. Emphasis should be placed on the reasons why you are applying to a program or seeking employment. You can include information about your experiences that are directly related to the position you are seeking and how they have prepared you for the challenges of the program and will enable you to be successful. Unlike a personal statement, you should not include any narrative about your personal background, such as personal illness that prompted you to consider a health professional career. It is acceptable to include your future plans, especially if you are applying to a residency, fellowship, or graduate program. The document should be prepared in a business letter format. You may want to consider discussing some of the following points in your letter:

- Discuss your career goals and ambitions.
- Describe the effectiveness of your communication skills including written, verbal, and/or interprofessional.
- Describe your leadership experiences that will benefit the program.
- Discuss your organization and time management skills.
- Provide examples of your ability to be resourceful and work independently.
- Discuss your research experience and your problem-solving skills.
- Outline your personal attributes, such as professionalism, maturity, cultural sensitivity, emotional stability, and dependability.
- Describe your practice experiences that will be an asset to the program.
- Discuss your experience in working with colleagues and teams.

Whether preparing a letter of intent or a personal statement, do your best to be original and stand out from the crowd. At the same time, you must come across as sincere—do not pretend to be the "ideal candidate." Avoid clichés and sycophantic comments such as "I want to help people," "I am a hard worker," or "I want to be a member of your nationally ranked and prestigious institution." Strive to avoid exaggeration and plagiarism. Ensure that your document is free of typographical, spelling, and grammatical errors. Most programs will use an evaluation rubric to assess personal statements and letters of intent. Because elements such as critical thinking, analysis, organization, theme development, language, and style will be evaluated, you should review your document and have peers and mentors review your document before its submission. Figure 3.2 is an example of a focused and effective letter of intent.

Evaluate your document and ask "Have I accomplished the following?"

- Adequately considered my intended audience
- Attracted the reader's attention with my opening paragraph
- Used proper grammar, punctuation, and tone
- Corrected spelling and typographical errors
- Been positive in discussing my theme(s)
- Highlighted my education and experience
- Been honest about my accomplishments
- Provided sufficient personal information
- Mentioned my short- and long-term goals

FIGURE 3.1 Sample personal statement.

Personal Statement

Miranda C. Stephens

As a child with asthma, I often went to the pharmacy with my parents to have my prescriptions filled. The pharmacist instructing me how to properly use my inhaler is my earliest memory of the career I wanted to pursue. During high school, I had the good fortune of being employed by an independent pharmacy owner in my home town. I dusted and stocked shelves, delivered prescriptions, and constantly observed the caring attitude of my employer. The independent pharmacy was a local gathering place for many individuals in our small town, especially for breakfast and lunch, and I was always impressed by the community's respect and trust in my employer. My resolve to become a pharmacist continued. When I expressed this desire to my employer, I was advised to pursue a science degree in college and to also prepare to become a pharmacy technician.

During my senior year of high school, I decided to attend the University of Georgia and major in biology, because the course work would fulfill the prerequisite courses for the school of pharmacy attended by my employer. I followed my employer's advice and paid attention to my studies, recognizing that admission to a school of pharmacy is competitive. I continued to work as a pharmacy technician during the winter and summer breaks to gain experience.

It was a proud day for me when I was accepted to the school of pharmacy I wanted to attend. My undergraduate study habits and discipline helped me become a successful student pharmacist. I was exposed to many facets of the profession during my four years of study as a Doctor of Pharmacy degree student. I was intrigued with the clinical role of the clinical pharmacist in a hospital setting, the consulting role of the pharmacist in a nursing home, and the research role of the pharmacist in academia and industry. However, during my advanced pharmacy practice rotations, I kept gravitating back to my interest in community pharmacy practice. At the same time, my leadership roles in my school's Academy of Student Pharmacists/American Pharmacists Association and Student Association of Community Pharmacists/National Community Pharmacists Association helped reinforce my interest in community pharmacy practice.

As graduation approached I realized that I definitely wanted to practice in a community pharmacy setting, preferably an independent community pharmacy. I am applying to your community pharmacy residency to fulfill my ultimate desire of becoming a successful community pharmacist practitioner. I recognize the need to expand my knowledge and expertise in providing patient care services and developing patient care programs in the community setting. I am confident that my passion for community pharmacy practice and my past experience will help me become a successful resident.

FIGURE 3.2 **Sample letter of intent.**

Jacob G. Cohen
121 West State Street
West Lafayette, Indiana 47906

May 10, 2017

Jason H. Johnson, Pharm.D.
Institute for Pharmaceutical Industry Fellowships
Ernest Mario School of Pharmacy
Rutgers, The State University of New Jersey
160 Frelinghuysen Road
Piscataway, NJ 08854

Dear Dr. Johnson:

I am writing to inform you of my interest in being considered for your industry fellowship program beginning July 1, 2017. At present, I am completing my Doctor of Pharmacy degree at the Purdue University College of Pharmacy.

During the past four years, I have explored various pharmacy practice settings through internships, pharmacy practice experiences, and research opportunities arranged by the school of pharmacy. I was professionally satisfied with each of these experiences, but I was most interested in those involving research and the pharmaceutical industry.

My initial industry experience began during the summer of 2015 when I was hired as an intern with Biologics, Inc. The internship experience involved rotations in the research, legal affairs, marketing and sales departments. I gained an understanding of the diverse opportunities available to pharmacists in the pharmaceutical industry.

During the 2015 academic year, I completed an elective course in pharmacoeconomics and a research project with Dr. Julia Fredricks. I found these experiences challenging and rewarding. I was able to arrange two elective advanced pharmacy practice rotations in the pharmaceutical industry and one rotation with the Food and Drug Administration during the final year of my Doctor of Pharmacy degree program. Each of these experiences helped me realize how much I enjoyed being associated with the pharmaceutical industry.

I have attached a copy of my curriculum vitae and a link to my website, which provides the details of my pharmaceutical industry experiences, including a summer internship; pharmacoeconomics research project; advanced pharmacy practice experiences; and my leadership involvement with our colleges Industry Pharmacist Organization chapter.

I look forward to the possibility of working with you.

Respectfully,

Jacob G. Cohen

CHAPTER 4

Preparing Your Résumé

Think of a résumé as a marketing tool that helps you land a job interview. Submitting a good résumé makes all the difference between it being read or thrown away. Employers are busy. When confronted with a stack of 100 résumés, they will zip through to find those that seem to represent positive professionals who have solid skills and can get things done.

In addition to documenting your education, experience, and accomplishments, a good résumé focuses on your positive attributes and how they potentially satisfy an employer's or program's needs. The trend in résumés has become increasingly "achievement oriented" to highlight job applicants' successes. Employers want to hire people who get results. By drawing attention to your unique talents and accomplishments instead of merely listing job descriptions, your résumé can show the value you have brought to your work and your professional activities. Put simply, résumés should be about the worker, not the work.

You should keep your résumé brief—usually one or two typewritten pages—and set it up so that potential employers can easily pick out key facts.

Although your résumé should reflect your individuality, most follow three basic formats, as outlined in the sidebar.

Basic Résumé Components

Résumés can contain many standard and optional sections, depending on your level of experience, areas of expertise, and the type of job you seek. The sidebar "Primary Elements of a Résumé" on the next page highlights these elements.

Three Common Résumé Formats

1. **Chronological Résumé.** This résumé format presents education and experience in reverse chronological order, with the most recent experience appearing first. The chronological résumé is usually organized by job titles and emphasizes positions you have held and the organizations where you have worked. The résumé of Page A. Shaw in Chapter 5 is an example of a chronological résumé.
2. **Functional or Skills Résumé.** This type of résumé is organized by the skills you have acquired through education and experience. The résumé focuses on what you want to do—the skills you hope to use in your new job—rather than what you have accomplished in the past. Functional résumés provide a good alternative when employment gaps exist or you have held many positions in a short time. The résumé of Gina Maria Ruiz in Chapter 5 is an example of a functional résumé.
3. **Combination Résumé.** This résumé style incorporates the best of both the functional and chronological formats. It includes both a description of positions you have held and a summary of skills you have acquired. The résumé of Amanda Ashley Sanderson in Chapter 5 provides an example of a combination résumé.

Although all three résumé formats are acceptable, it is a safe bet to select the style that most people within your profession use. In the pharmacy community, the chronological résumé is used most often.

Primary Elements of a Résumé

- Contact information
- Summary statement (optional)
- Career objective (optional)
- Education
- Experience
- Memberships and service
- Awards and honors

Other Potential Elements

- Licenses and certificates
- Committees
- Personal interests or activities
- Research interests
- Publications, editorships, presentations
- Special skills
- Special training and continuing education
- Leadership positions
- References

Contact Information

Always begin your résumé with your contact information, including name, address, telephone number, and e-mail address. Use either your full legal name or your first name, middle initial, and last name. Do not put the term "résumé" at the top. Instead, use your name as the title.

Individuals with two addresses—a situation that is especially common among students—should list both addresses and related contact information to minimize the chance of communication gaps. You do not want to compromise your chances of landing an interview or a position simply because the employer could not reach you.

Career Objective

Including a career objective on your résumé is considered optional by recruitment experts. Many pharmacists and other health professionals omit career statements from their résumés. If you choose to include one, be sure your objective is clearly stated. Some people fear that including a career objective on their résumé will give too narrow a view of their interests. When written properly, however, a career statement can highlight how your experience and skills relate to the position you desire.

Basically, a career objective provides a brief, clear statement detailing the type of position you want and how your skills qualify you for the job. Directly echoing the needs of an employer or a program director will increase the likelihood that your résumé will be considered for further review. Chapter 1 provides several examples of career objectives.

When writing your statement, avoid generic phrases such as "seeking a position with opportunity for advancement" or "seeking a challenging position for professional growth." Most importantly, make sure your career statement closely matches the position you seek.

Summary Statement

In addition to a career objective, you can also include a summary statement on your résumé. A summary statement highlights your unique abilities or experiences that a reviewer might not easily detect in a quick review of your résumé. Place your summary statement directly after your career objective.

Opinions vary on the value of summary statements. Although many health professionals do not include them, use of these statements is growing in most other sectors. A well-written, effective summary is a snapshot of your background, quickly focusing readers on the essence of your résumé and compelling them to continue on to the details. Some people in hiring positions say they like the way summary statements quickly call attention to key strengths. If you use a summary statement, however, the material in the rest of your résumé must back up its assertions. For example, if you claim to have leadership skills, the experience and accomplishments cited in the body of your résumé must show that you have taken initiatives, headed groups, and motivated others.

Academic Standing

Recent graduates often include information about their academic standing in the education section of their résumé. Some list a cumulative grade point average or class standing, especially if they have been an "A" or "B" student. Others rely on a statement about their graduation honor to convey their academic success (e.g., graduated cum laude). Although including this information is an excellent approach, keep in mind that different colleges and universities may define grade points for graduation honors differently. For example, out of a possible 4.0 cumulative grade point average, cum laude may range from 3.3 to 3.59; magna cum laude from 3.5 to 3.89; and summa cum laude from 3.8 to 4.0.

Education

Educational experience provides employers with critical information. List relevant courses, and provide the name and location of the institution, dates of attendance, and the type of degree earned. If you are still pursuing a degree, list the date that you expect to earn the degree (e.g., "degree expected May 2007"). You can use the term "degree in progress" if you do not know your expected date of graduation.

If you took only one or two courses at a college or university to fulfill a degree requirement, you usually do not need to list that institution. Similarly, do not include high school credentials unless you have attended college for less than two years.

If you include high school information in your educational experience, list the relevant information immediately after the college education information (reverse chronological order), and state the school's name and location, dates of attendance, and diploma earned.

Pre-pharmacy students and technician candidates who do not have a college degree but have completed college courses relevant to an available position (e.g., chemistry or biology courses) can consider listing them under a heading such as "relevant course work."

Common headings for the education section include "education and professional training" or "academic degrees and postgraduate training." Here you can include such programs as residencies, fellowships, or technician training programs. You should list the programs in reverse chronological order, and supply the name and location of the institution, dates of attendance, and the type of certificate or credential earned. Provide the name of the program director or major preceptor, as well as the accreditation status of the program, if desired.

Some people like to include their professional training as a separate section, especially if they have completed a residency or specialized program that they want to highlight. This inclusion usually depends on personal preference. Sometimes the final decision comes down to how much space you have on the page.

Professional Experience

Employers focus sharply on the experience section of the résumé. In the early stages of your career you may find this section challenging to prepare, because your professional experiences may include work outside the profession. As your career develops and you acquire more experience, you can fill this section with pharmacy-related professional work.

Information about your experience should include the name and location of the agency or institution; beginning and ending dates of service; title of the position held; and a description of key duties that uses active, energetic phrasing and cites accomplishments. Be selective—highlight responsibilities that demonstrate initiative and special skills as opposed to listing each item on your job description. When detailing positions and related accomplishments, make your statements clear, concise, and action oriented. Organize your material in a brief narrative or short bullet statements. Use the present tense to describe your current job and past tense for previous jobs.

How you organize the experience section of your résumé depends on the type of résumé you prepare.

Chronological Résumés

In chronological résumés—commonly used by pharmacy professionals—you start with your most recent position. Listing each position in reverse chronological order helps accentuate a consistent pattern of employment. When using this format, however, you may need to omit part-time or short-term positions. If you are concerned about a potential employer's reaction to "employment gaps," go ahead and list your part-time or short-term employment.

Functional Résumés

In functional résumés, you organize the experience section according to skills that relate to the position sought. When using this format, make sure you also include employers, position titles, and years of experience.

Combination Résumés

A combination of the chronological and functional résumés allows for creativity and individuality. For example, you can list employers in a chronological fashion while including the various skills acquired with each employer.

Volunteer Experience

In the experience section of your résumé, you can also include volunteer experience, especially if you have sustained your commitment for a year or more and you have demonstrated an ability to apply the knowledge and skills gained. The experience gained through volunteerism, especially in an activity related to health care, can provide as much value as experience acquired through a paid position.

Special Skills

Highlighting your special skills—such as experience with specific computer software or laboratory equipment—may give you a unique advantage in competing for a position. Some people create a heading in the résumé titled "special skills" to accentuate this information. You can also include a heading such as "licenses and certificates" for professional licenses (pharmacist, pharmacy intern) and certificates (pharmacy technician, cardiopulmonary resuscitation training, Board of

Pharmacy Specialties certification) if you have not included this information elsewhere in your résumé.

Memberships and Service

Include memberships and service roles in your résumé, especially those related to professional activities. In addition to years of membership, list any offices held or specific recognition gained that demonstrates your potential leadership ability. This section is also a good place to document community service activities.

Awards and Honors

List any awards, honors, or other recognition you have received. If you have earned several accolades, you may want to create a special section for them. Otherwise, list them somewhere else in your résumé. For example, you could include a service award in the activities section of your résumé or major grants in the research section. Although such information usually appears in the curriculum vitae, it may help to highlight a significant grant award or published research article in your résumé.

References

References should not appear on the résumé unless the prospective employer specifically requests them. They take up valuable space and may differ depending on the position you seek. Some résumés include the statement "references available upon request" at the bottom of the last page, but this statement is optional.

Prepare a separate sheet with references for potential employers. The reference sheet should fill no more than a single page and should include the name, affiliation, mailing address, and telephone number for each reference. If you have a reference's fax number and e-mail address, include them as well. You can also include a brief statement about what each reference can contribute about your knowledge, skills, and abilities. Before listing references, check with each person for permission.

When potential employers contact references, they may ask questions orally or request a written assessment of your abilities. Table 4.1 lists common questions that potential employers may ask your references.

Military Service and Other Sections

Because résumés highlight your knowledge, skills, and abilities, you may need to create unique sections to accommodate your background. For example, if you served in the military, you should include information about the branch of service; provide entry and discharge dates; and prepare a reverse chronological listing that highlights your rank, type of discharge, and reserves activity.

TABLE 4.1 Questions to Ask Applicant's References

How long have you known the individual and in what capacity?
How well do you know the applicant?
What is your estimate of the applicant's academic ability?
Can the applicant apply his or her knowledge and skills?
How would you describe the quality of the applicant's work?
How would you rate the applicant's written communication skills?
How would you rate the applicant's verbal communication skills?
Is the applicant dependable and reliable?
Does the applicant complete assignments on time?
Does the applicant exercise good judgment?
Is the applicant willing to accept constructive criticism?
How would you assess the applicant's creativity and ability to solve problems?
Does the applicant display enthusiasm?
Does the applicant demonstrate the ability to organize and manage time in an efficient manner?
Is the applicant a leader?
How would you describe the applicant's emotional stability and level of maturity?
How would you rate the applicant's motivation?
How would you rate the applicant's initiative?
How would you rate the applicant's assertiveness?
What is your impression of the applicant's integrity?
Does the applicant demonstrate the ability to work effectively with peers?
Is the applicant committed to professional practice?
What is the applicant's reputation as a pharmacy practitioner?
What is the applicant's reputation as a researcher?
Does the applicant exhibit effective administrative and management skills?
What is the applicant's reputation as a teacher?
What do you consider the applicant's strengths?
What do you consider the applicant's weaknesses?
What is your overall assessment of the applicant?
Do you know of anything that would disqualify the applicant from further consideration?
Can you think of anything I should know about the applicant that I have not asked?

Source: Criscito P. *Résumés in Cyberspace.* Colorado Springs, CO: ProType, Ltd.; 1997:83.

Other Résumé Considerations

Order of Sections

The order of your résumé sections will vary on an individual basis. Typically, pharmacy professionals start with general information and proceed to education, experience, activities, honors, and references. Optional sections include career objective, statement of qualifications, relevant course work, and special skills.

Formatting and Readability of Text

A successful résumé should appeal to the reader's eye. It should be neat, well organized, and easily readable with clear, consistent headers. For good readability, follow these specifications:

- White, off-white, or light ivory paper with a bond weight of 20 or 24 pounds
- Font size of 10 to 14 points
- Consistent typeface
- Consistent line spacing
- One-inch margins at the top, sides, and bottom of page
- Section headings and breaks between sections
- Consistent format so that the typed copy and white space look symmetrical
- Quality printer with black ink

Length of Résumé

Recruiters and busy personnel assistants tend to favor one-page résumés. If you do not have a lot of professional experience, one page will probably suffice. However, if you have a significant background in pharmacy, you may need to add a second page. Anyone with more than a two-page résumé should consider preparing a curriculum vitae, which is detailed in Chapter 6.

Selection of Paper

The type of paper you use can make a difference, so opt for better quality paper when possible. Look for business stationery with a bond weight of 20 or 24 pounds and more cotton fiber than that in regular photocopy paper. Many office supply stores carry paper products specifically labeled as "letterhead and résumé paper" that you can use with laser or ink jet printers.

Use of Action Verbs

When describing your experiences and accomplishments, use action verbs and avoid excessive wordiness. For example, instead of "vaccines were administered," say "administered vaccines" and rather than "had responsibility for counseling patients," say "counseled patients."

Action verbs are your ally as you underscore your achievements. You should never stretch the truth, but by all means state your activities in the best possible light. "Created" sounds much more impressive than "began," for example. Words such as "worked on" or "handled" can be replaced with "produced," "developed," or "prepared." Table 4.2 lists commonly used action verbs in pharmacy-related résumés.

TABLE 4.2 Action Verbs

A	Assured	Changed	Cooperated	Displayed	Exhibited	Greeted
Accepted	Attained	Checked	Coordinated	Distributed	Expanded	Guided
Accomplished	Attended	Chose	Corrected	Documented	Expedited	
Achieved	Audited	Classified	Corresponded	Drafted	Experimented	**H**
Acquired	Authored	Collaborated	Counseled		Explained	Handled
Addressed	Authorized	Collated	Created	**E**	Extended	Hired
Adjusted	Automated	Collected	Critiqued	Edited	Extracted	Hosted
Administered	Awarded	Communicated		Educated		
Advanced		Compared	**D**	Eliminated	**F**	**I**
Advised	**B**	Compiled	Debated	Employed	Facilitated	Identified
Aided	Balanced	Completed	Decided	Enabled	Familiarized	Illustrated
Allocated	Briefed	Compounded	Decreased	Enacted	Filed	Implemented
Analyzed	Budgeted	Computed	Defined	Encouraged	Finalized	Improved
Answered	Built	Computerized	Delegated	Enforced	Focused	Incorporated
Applied		Conceptualized	Delivered	Enhanced	Followed	Increased
Appointed	**C**	Conducted	Demonstrated	Enlisted	Forecasted	Indexed
Appraised	Calculated	Conferred	Described	Enrolled	Formalized	Individualized
Apprised	Calibrated	Consolidated	Designed	Entered	Formed	Influenced
Appropriated	Captured	Constructed	Detected	Ensured	Formulated	Informed
Approved	Cared for	Consulted	Determined	Established	Funded	Initiated
Arranged	Catalogued	Contacted	Developed	Estimated	Furnished	Inspected
Assembled	Centralized	Contracted	Devised	Evaluated		Installed
Assessed	Certified	Contributed	Directed	Examined	**G**	Instituted
Assigned	Chaired	Controlled	Discovered	Exceeded	Gained	Instructed
Assisted	Charted	Converted	Dispensed	Executed	Generated	Integrated

(continues on next page)

TABLE 4.2 Action Verbs ***(continued)***

Interacted
Interfaced
Interpreted
Interviewed
Introduced
Invented
Inventoried
Investigated
Issued
Itemized

J
Joined
Judged
Justified

L
Launched
Lectured
Led
Lessened
Located

M
Maintained
Managed
Manufactured
Marketed
Mastered
Measured
Mediated
Mentored
Merged
Met
Modeled
Moderated
Modernized
Modified
Monitored
Motivated

N
Negotiated
Nominated
Notified

O
Observed
Obtained
Operated
Ordered
Organized
Oriented
Originated
Outlined
Outsourced

P
Packaged
Participated
Patented
Performed
Persuaded
Planned
Prepared
Presented
Presided
Prevented
Printed
Prioritized
Processed
Procured
Produced
Programmed
Projected
Promoted
Proposed
Provided
Publicized
Published
Purchased

Q
Qualified
Quantified

R
Received
Recognized
Recommended
Reconciled
Recorded
Recruited
Redesigned
Reduced
Reengineered
Referred
Registered
Regulated
Released
Reorganized
Replied
Reported
Represented
Requested
Researched
Resolved
Responded
Retrieved
Reviewed
Revised
Revitalized

S
Saved
Scanned
Scheduled
Screened
Searched
Secured
Selected
Served
Shaped
Simplified
Solved
Sorted
Sought
Specified
Sponsored
Staffed
Standardized
Stimulated
Streamlined
Strengthened
Structured
Studied
Submitted
Summarized
Supervised
Supplied
Supported
Surveyed

T
Tabulated
Taught
Tested
Traced
Trained
Transcribed
Transferred
Translated
Transmitted
Tutored
Typed

U
Undertook
Updated
Upgraded
Utilized

V
Validated
Verified
Volunteered

W
Worked
Wrote

Electronic Résumé Formats

In today's high-tech world a lot of information is sent over the internet, so you will need versions of your résumé that are suitable for scanning and electronic transmission. Some employers or program directors may want to scan your résumé so they can store it in an electronic database and quickly route it to those who will be involved in reviewing your application. This means you need to modify your résumé to minimize the loss of content.

Preparing a Scannable Résumé

To accommodate the limited optical character recognition technology associated with typical scanning devices, make sure your résumé text is crystal clear and the letters do not touch one another. Although serif fonts such as Bookman, Courier, and Times New Roman are easier for the eye to read, sans serif fonts scan better, because they lack the decorative marks at the end of the character strokes. Table 4.3 provides a comparison of fonts.

Avoid using graphics, borders, lines, underlining, shading, boldface type, bullets, italics, brackets, and parentheses. To further minimize the chance of lost content, do not fold a résumé unless the creases avoid the lines of type. If your résumé exceeds one page, include your name on the second page and do not staple the pages.

Preparing an Electronic Résumé

The same guidelines outlined for scanned résumés apply when preparing an electronic résumé. Usually, electronic

TABLE 4.3 Sample Font Types

Serif	
Bookman Old Style	asdfjklm ASDFJKLM 123
Garamond	asdfjklm ASDFJKLM 123
Georgia	asdfjklm ASDFJKLM 123
Times New Roman	asdfjklm ASDFJKLM 123
Sans Serif	
Arial	asdfjklm ASDFJKLM 123
Helvetica	asdfjklm ASDFJKLM 123
Lucida Sans	asdfjklm ASDFJKLM 123
Tahoma	asdfjklm ASDFJKLM 123
Verdana	asdfjklm ASDFJKLM 123

résumés are submitted by e-mail, through a web page, or by completion of an electronic form.

When preparing an electronic résumé, use the Adobe Acrobat portable document format, or PDF, file. A PDF file transmits a document exactly as it was prepared, so a potential employer can view and print it on any system. To prepare PDF files, use Adobe Acrobat software or Microsoft Office Programs. If you want only to view PDF files without the ability to create them, you can download a free copy of Adobe Reader from http://www.adobe.com. Regardless of the file type you use, test the appearance of the final copy by sending the completed electronic résumé to your e-mail address.

Résumé Don'ts

When developing your résumé, do not include the following personal information:

- Social Security number
- Age
- Gender
- Marital status or spouse's name
- Health status or disabilities
- Children's names and ages
- Height and weight
- Race, ethnic background, or religion

Key Words

To make electronic and scanned résumés more effective, you may need to include key words or phrases that match those specified by an employer or a program director. Although searching for key words is not a common practice, the process is used when a large number of applications have been received for a highly competitive position. Try to include as many key words as possible in descriptions of your skills and qualifications. You may even want to consider a résumé section that lists all key words, especially those related to skills. Table 4.4 lists common key words for pharmacy-related electronic résumés.

TABLE 4.4 Key Pharmacy-Related Words

A
Accreditation
Administration
Administrative support
Adverse drug reaction
Advertising
Alternative medicine
Alumni relations
Ambulatory care
Aseptic technique
Audits

B
Benchmarking
Biologicals
Biotechnology
Budget administration
Budget allocation

C
Career development
Case management
Certification
Change management
Clinical decision making
Clinical research
Clinical services
Clinical services management
Clinical studies
Communication
Community outreach
Community practice
Compensation
Competitive bidding
Compounding
Computer systems
Computers
Continuity of care
Continuous quality improvement
Contract administration
Contract negotiations
Controlled substances
Corporate sponsorship
Correspondence
Contract administration
Cost avoidance
Cost reduction
Credentialing
Curriculum development
Customer relations
Customer satisfaction
Customer service

D
Data collection
Disease management program
Dispensing devices
Distribution
Documentation
Drug administration
Drug distribution
Drug distribution automation
Drug distribution system
Drug evaluation
Drug information
Drug interactions
Drug metabolism
Drug therapy monitoring
Drug usage evaluation
Drug use control
Drug utilization

E
Economics
Educational programming
Equipment
Errors
Ethics

F
Financial management
Formulary
Formulation
Full time equivalent
Fundraising

G
Geriatrics
Good manufacturing practices
Government affairs
Grant administration
Guidelines

H
Health maintenance organization
Health care system
Health promotion
Home health care
Hospice care
Hospital

I
Immunization
Immunology
Improving health outcomes
Incompatibilities
Industry
Industry relations
Infectious diseases
Information systems
Injections
Inpatient care
Instructional media
Internal medicine

(continues on next page)

TABLE 4.4 Key Pharmacy-Related Words *(continued)*

Interventions
Intravenous therapy
Inventory control
Investigational drug

J
The Joint Commission
Just-in-time inventory

L
Labeling
Leadership development
Leadership training
Legislation
Long-term care

M
Mail order services
Managed care
Marketing
Manufacturing
Market research
Materials management
Media relations
Medication errors
Medication use evaluation
Meeting planning

N
Needs assessment
Not-for-profit
Nuclear pharmacy
Nursing home
Nutrition
Nutrition support

O
Office management
Office services
Oncology
Operating budget
Order processing
Outcomes
Outcomes research
Outsourcing
Over-the-counter drugs

P
Packaging
Pain management
Patient care
Patient counseling
Patient information
Patient relations
Pediatrics
Peer review
Performance appraisal
Personnel
Pharmaceutical care
Pharmaceutical technology
Pharmaceutics
Pharmacodynamics
Pharmacoeconomics
Pharmacoepidemiology
Pharmacogenetics
Pharmacogenomics
Pharmacognosy
Pharmacokinetics
Pharmacology
Pharmacopeial standards
Pharmacotherapy
Pharmacy benefit management
Pharmacy practice
Poison control
Policy and procedures
Policy development
Political affairs
Practice management
Prescribing
Prescription benefit management
Prescriptions
Pricing
Primary care
Procurement
Product development
Product selection
Productivity
Productivity improvement
Professional competence
Professional recruitment
Project management
Project planning
Protocols
Psychiatric pharmacy
Public affairs
Public health
Public policy development
Purchasing

Q
Quality assurance
Quality control
Quality improvement
Quality of care
Quality of life

R
Records management
Recruitment and retention
Reengineering
Research and development
Reimbursement
Request for proposal
Research
Resource management
Regulatory affairs
Retail sales
Risk management

S
Scheduling
Service delivery
Specialty
Speaker's bureau
Staffing
Standards
Strategic planning
Sterile products
Substance abuse

T
Team building
Team leadership
Technical support
Therapeutic efficacy
Therapeutic equivalency
Therapeutic substitution
Third party payer

U
Unit dose
Utilization review

V
Vaccines
Vendor relations
Volunteer recruitment
Volunteer training

W
Wellness program
Workload

Tips, Checklists, and Sample Résumés

CHAPTER 5

When selecting your résumé's content and format, keep in mind what you want to accomplish as well as what the business and professional communities expect. "Anything goes" does not apply. Instead, follow tried-and-true formats, and use standard headings and patterns of organization.

This chapter provides examples of effective résumés, tips for format and approach, and advice about problems to avoid. The checklists should help you evaluate your résumé to ensure you have included key elements and have not made mistakes that will detract from your résumé's impact. In addition, Table 5.1 lists commonly used résumé headings and subheadings.

Checklist of Résumé Design Elements

- Try to keep the length to one page, and definitely do not exceed two pages.
- Use a high-quality bond paper in white, off-white, or light ivory.
- Position the watermark, if present, on the top side of the paper for printing.
- Use a quality laser jet printer.
- Use only one side of each page for printing.
- Ensure that typed copy appears symmetrical on the page.
- Achieve a reasonable balance between typed copy and white space to avoid having a page that looks overcrowded.
- Maintain one-inch margins at the top, bottom, and sides of the document.
- Justify the left margin.
- Avoid the use of graphics.

Format

Your résumé format will vary depending on whether you need a standard, scannable, or electronic résumé. Several factors can help make your résumé readable and pleasing to the eye. Use the provided checklist to ensure you have incorporated the key design elements into your résumé.

The Standard Résumé

Keep a standard résumé as a permanent file or hard copy, even if you primarily send out electronic versions. Without the limitations imposed by electronic transmission and scanning, you will have more format flexibility. Even so, adhere to the design guidelines in the Checklist for Standard Résumés.

Checklist for Standard Résumés

- Choose a font and use it consistently: serif font (e.g., Bookman Old Style, Garamond, Georgia, Times New Roman) or a sans serif font (e.g., Arial, Helvetica, Lucida Sans, Tahoma, Verdana).
- Use a font size between 10 and 14 points.
- Limit the number of font sizes to no more than three.
- Use various design elements (e.g., bullets, lines, italic type, boldface type, shading) to create a unique appearance, but do not overuse them.

Tip: Use design elements such as boldface type, bullets, lines, and italics judiciously. Do not use graphics in your résumé. And most importantly, make sure your résumé has no typographical, grammatical, or spelling errors.

TABLE 5.1 Useful Headings for Résumés and CVs

Career Goal	Goal, Objective, Career Objective, Position Objective
Summary of Qualifications	Profile, qualifications profile, career profile, professional profile, career highlights, professional accomplishments, achievements, key achievements, highlights of achievements, synopsis
Education	Academic preparation, educational background, educational and professional training, education and specialized training, education and professional development, academic degrees and postgraduate training
Thesis	Dissertation, dissertation title, master's project Note: Consider "thesis" as a separate heading if it is not included in the education section.
Training	Specialized training, postgraduate training, residency, residency experience, fellowship, fellowship experience, postdoctoral experience, mentoring Note: Consider "training" as a separate heading if postgraduate training is not included in the education or experience sections.
Experience	Highlights of experience, employment experience, employment, employment history, work history, professional experience, pharmacy practice experience, professional highlights and achievements, experience and accomplishments, professional background, experience summary. Possible subheadings: internships, clerkships (e.g., completed, scheduled), residency rotations (e.g., completed, scheduled, concurrent, longitudinal), experiential learning, professional development, clinical experience, related experience, other work experience, externships (i.e., advanced pharmacy practice experience rotations), positions held
Special Skills	Technical skills, technology skills, computer skills, equipment knowledge and skills, computer proficiency, computer software proficiency
Licenses and Certificates	Credentials, licenses, licensure, professional licensure, certificates, certifications, licensure and certifications, professional registration, professional certifications, special training Note: Include skills that are relevant but outside the general body of pharmacy skills.
Research Experience	Research, grants, contracts, grants and contracts, grants and contracts (approved and funded), grants and contracts, (approved, not funded), research funding applications, grants reviewed, review panel experience, patents, theses committees, dissertation committees, postdoctoral resident supervision, postdoctoral residency preceptorship, postdoctoral residents, postdoctoral fellow supervision, postdoctoral fellows, graduate students supervised, laboratory research experience, clinical research experience, research coordination and direction, research supervision, scholarship, scholarship experience, projects, major research interests, research interests
Academic Appointments	Teaching experience, instruction, course participation, courses taught, courses developed, courses developed and taught, graduate course participation, professional course participation, course highlights, areas of expertise, areas of concentration, peer-reviewed continuing education, extramural lecture experience
Administrative Experience	Personnel management, fiscal management, supervisory experience

TABLE 5.1 Useful Headings for Résumés and CVs *(continued)*

Publications	Recent publications, publications in peer-reviewed journals, selected publications, scholarly works, review articles, monographs Possible subheadings: textbook chapters, books, monographs, books and monographs, articles in refereed journals, editorials, films, audiotapes, computer simulations, self-instructional programs, creative works, bibliographies, review articles, published proceedings, published abstracts, abstracts, manuscripts submitted for publication, editorial boards, editorial activities, journal referee, miscellaneous publications
Presentations	Invited presentations, recent presentations, poster presentations, invited lectures, invited papers and lectures, research papers presented at national meetings, seminars presented, scholarly presentations, conference presentations, workshops
Affiliations	Memberships, professional memberships, professional affiliations, professional associations, professional and community affiliations, professional societies, membership in professional organizations Note: Appointments and offices held may be included with the listing of respective affiliations.
Leadership Experience	Appointments and offices held, committee leadership, professional association leadership Possible subheadings: name of the affiliation, followed by appointments and offices held
Consulting Experience	Consulting, consultation, consulting projects, consultantships, consulting activity
Service Activities	Community service, volunteer service, volunteerism, volunteer work, community involvement, community and volunteer activities, academic service, public service, professional service, academic service and committee activity, committee activity (e.g., national, university, school or college, department or division, association)
Professional Development	Postgraduate professional development Possible subheadings: continuing education, meetings attended, courses attended, seminars and symposia attended, conferences attended
Military Experience	Military service
Awards and Honors	Honors and distinctions, distinctions, accomplishments and awards, academic achievements, academic awards, academic honors, special honors, special recognition, selected achievements, awards and fellowships, scholarships, prizes
Personal Interests	Leisure activities, sports activities, hobbies Note: Include these headings only if they have some uniqueness or bearing on the position.
References	

Scannable Résumé

To make your résumé suitable for scanning, you will need to alter the format to accommodate the use of optical character recognition technology. The Checklist for Scannable Résumés lists some general guidelines to follow.

Do's and Don'ts of Résumé Writing

DO:

- Use a consistent format throughout your résumé.
- Use either your full legal name or your first name, middle initial, and last name.
- Arrange experience according to a chronological, functional, or combination format.
- List positions in reverse chronological order.
- Include accurate position titles.
- Use the present tense to describe your current work and the past tense to describe previous positions.
- Quantify your accomplishments whenever you can (number of procedures, increases in services, amount of budget, etc).
- Describe skills using phrases with action verbs.
- Emphasize achievements rather than providing a laundry list of duties.
- Consider highlighting special skills with a unique heading.
- Identify the title, sponsor, and date of significant recognition or awards.
- Write out numbers between one and nine, and use numerals for 10 and above.
- Use a consistent format for telephone numbers and dates.
- If abbreviating names of states, use the proper two-letter abbreviations.
- Proofread the document for grammar, spelling, syntax, and punctuation errors.

DON'T:

- Use the word "Résumé" as the document's heading.
- Use vague descriptions.
- Exaggerate your responsibilities or accomplishments.
- Use jargon, unfamiliar abbreviations, or slang.
- Allow any typographical, spelling, or grammatical errors.
- List your references on the résumé.

Electronic Résumé

Résumés suitable for sending electronically must undergo further modifications than scannable résumés because of inconsistencies in hardware components and software programs. The sidebar "Checklist for Electronic Résumés" lists some guidelines for creating electronic résumés.

Federal Résumé

The guidelines for preparing a résumé for a United States government position differ from those for other types of positions. A federal résumé is more detailed, and in many cases it will exceed the usual two-page limit, because greater documentation of your skill set, past duties, and accomplishments is needed. A guide to preparing a federal résumé can be found at http://www.archives.gov/careers/jobs/forms/resume-guide.pdf.

Helpful Hints

When you prepare your résumé, adhering to the following guidelines will help you avoid many common mistakes.

Résumé Headings

Generally, you do not need a heading for your contact information. Depending on the complexity of the information; however, labels such as the following can sometimes help.

- Addresses and telephone numbers
- Permanent address
- Temporary address
- Employment address
- Office
- Home

Table 5.1 lists commonly used résumé headings and subheadings. You can use this list as a guide in selecting the most appropriate headings for your résumé.

Spell Checking

Do not forget to check your document for spelling errors before saving it as a text file. Use the "spell check" function on your word-processing program, but do not rely on it alone. Read each word carefully.

Proofreading

Before proofreading your own work, put it aside for a day or two. After that, you can read it again with fresh eyes. Printing an electronic copy often can enhance your proofreading. Some people find it helpful to proofread backwards, starting with the last word and moving in reverse order to the first word. Or you can ask a friend or colleague to proofread your résumé for you. Pay special attention to headings, because most errors in this area are overlooked.

Sample Résumés

On the following pages, you will find examples of résumés for pharmacy professionals that contain comments about their features. Although good résumés follow certain general rules, there are no absolutes and no particular style is right for everyone.

The most important thing is to make sure your résumé lets your strengths shine through. In the 15 seconds or so that decision makers—whether pharmacists or human resources specialists—spend skimming each applicant's materials to decide whether to consider him or her for an interview, ask yourself "Will they be able to identify my substantive skills and achievements?"

A final word of caution about résumés: always be truthful. Although you need to portray yourself in the best possible light, saying you directed a blood pressure screening when all you did was show up and watch or published a paper that does not even exist will come back to haunt you in the interview.

Checklist for Electronic Résumés

In addition to using the guidelines provided for scannable résumés, do the following when preparing an electronic résumé:

- Use capital letters as a replacement for boldface type or underlining in heads and subheads.
- Save the final document in a suitable format for electronic transmission (e.g., HTML for internet posting and PDF for attaching to an e-mail).

Checklist for Scannable Résumés

- Choose a consistent sans serif font.
- Avoid folding and stapling the résumé.
- Save the final version of a document file as text only, rich text format, or PDF.
- Minimize the use of design elements (e.g., bullets, lines, underlining, italics, boldface type, brackets, parentheses, shading).
- Create spaces using the spacebar and avoid the use of tabs.
- Use hard carriage returns at the end of each line.
- Do not use word wrapping.
- Include key words related to the skills included in a computer search strategy (Table 4.4).
- Use a font size between 12 and 14 points.
- Include your name on the second page.
- Maintain one-inch margins at the top, bottom, and sides of the document.
- Justify the left margin.
- Avoid the use of graphics.

RÉSUMÉ 1 Ashley Brooke Foster

A chronological résumé for a pharmacy technician and chemistry student looking for a position in a community pharmacy. Font: Times New Roman 12 point.

Ashley Brooke Foster

Local Address
9501 Rio Verde Way
Tucson, Arizona 85710
(480) 451-8142
E-mail:abfoster@u.arizona.edu

Permanent Address
3301 Thorntree Road
Scottsville, Arizona 85260
(520) 290-7721

Objective helps employers focus quickly on what this candidate is looking for.

OBJECTIVE:	To obtain a pharmacy technician position in a community pharmacy.	
EDUCATION:	University of Arizona Tucson, Arizona Major: B.S. in Chemistry	August 2015 – Present Graduation Anticipated: 2019 G.P.A.: 3.4 / 4.0
	Chaparral High School Scottsville, Arizona	September 2011 – May 2015
EXPERIENCE:	Hazleton Realtors Scottsville, Arizona Receptionist	June 2015 – August 2015
	Johnson Floral Designs Scottsville, Arizona Sales Associate	May 2014 – August 2014
	Verda Country Club Scottsville, Arizona Lifeguard	June 2013 – August 2013
	Mary Immaculate Hospital Scottsville, Arizona Volunteer (4-20 Hours/Week)	July 2012 – December 2014
CERTIFICATES:	American Red Cross First Aid Certificate American Red Cross Adult CPR Certificate American Red Cross Infant & Child CPR	2013 – 2016 2013 – 2016 2013 – 2016
MEMBERSHIPS:	Student Affiliates of the American Chemical Society and Chemistry Club, University of Arizona	2015 – Present

This section does an effective job of concisely highlighting achievements.

Actual résumé size is 8.5 x 11 inches.

RÉSUMÉ 2 Page A. Shaw

A chronological résumé for a pharmacy technician attending college part time.
Font: Arial Narrow 12 and 10 point.

Format is simple and clean.

Page A. Shaw
3321 Guyton Way, Apartment 32A
Jacksonville, Florida 32225
904/645-9729

EDUCATION

September 2012 – Present (Part-time)	University of North Florida College of Arts and Sciences Jacksonville, Florida Completed 44 Semester Hours
September 2008 – May 2012	Providence High School Jacksonville, Florida

Here she lists positions held and general duties. More emphasis on key achievements would help employers quickly identify what strengths she would offer them.

WORK EXPERIENCE

July 2012 – Present	CVS, Jacksonville, FL Pharmacy Technician Assisted pharmacists in performing tasks and duties related to dispensing prescription medications
May 2011 – August 2011	Sunshine Gallery, Inc., Atlantic Beach, FL Customer Service Clerk Sold, matted and framed art work
May 2010 – August 2010	Jackson and Associates, Atlantic Beach, FL Secretarial Assistant Performed general administrative tasks
May 2009 – September 2009	Leed's Department Store, Jacksonville, FL Sales Associate Responsible for the sale of children's clothing

COMPUTER SKILLS

Microsoft Office

ORGANIZATIONS

January 2013 – Present	Pre-Medical Profession's Program University of North Florida

REFERENCES

Provided upon request

This statement is optional and can easily be omitted if space for more critical information is needed.

Actual résumé size is 8.5 x 11 inches.

RÉSUMÉ 3 Michael Patrick Garrett

Chronological résumé of a certified pharmacy technician enrolled in a pre-pharmacy course of study.
Font: Arial 12 point.

MICHAEL PATRICK GARRETT

804-A Westside Avenue • Iowa City, Iowa 52240 • 319.358.5107
E-mail: mpgarret@uiowa.edu
www.linkedin.com/in/mpgarrett

> Objective is concise and direct.

OBJECTIVE Pharmacy technician position in a health-system pharmacy

EDUCATION

August 2015–Present
University of Iowa
Iowa City, Iowa
Major: Pre-Pharmacy

> Pay attention to details. The font switch here is inconsistent with the rest of the format.

September 2014–May 2015
Grand View College
Des Moines, Iowa

WORK EXPERIENCE

June 2015–August 2015
Pharmacy Technician
Albertsons Pharmacy
Des Moines, Iowa
Supervisor: Ted Hankle, R.Ph.
319.785.6700

> This résumé has plenty of extra space to include a few key duties and accomplishments. Readers get no sense of this candidate's top attributes. Being a groundskeeper, for example, may call for initiative and problem-solving skills.

May 2010–August 2014 (Summers)
Groundskeeper
Deer Valley Golf Club
Des Moines, Iowa
Supervisor: James Simpson
319.472.8739

CERTIFICATION Certified Pharmacy Technician awarded July 2015

HONORS

Dean's List, Grand View College, Spring 2015
Eagle Scout, Mid-Iowa Council, 2007

> These honors suggest the candidate has leadership abilities, but he missed the opportunity to elaborate.

Actual résumé size is 8.5 x 11 inches.

RÉSUMÉ 4 Minh T. Ngo

Chronological résumé of a pharmacy technician who wants to attend pharmacy school.
Font: Times New Roman 12 point.

MINH T. NGO

5231 Warfield Drive
Oakland, California 94611
(510) 339-5416

> This person seems to have a lot of initiative, but merely listing jobs and volunteer work does not showcase this attribute.

EXPERIENCE

June 2015–Present	Pharmacy Technician	Bayside Pharmacy Oakland, CA
May 2014–August 2014	Pharmacy Technician	Providence Hospital Oakland, CA
June 2013–August 2013	Bank Teller	Wells Fargo Bank Berkeley, CA
July 2011–December 2014 (10–30 Hours/Week)	Waiter/Cook	Great Wall Restaurant Berkeley, CA

EDUCATION

September 2011–June 2015	Freemont High School Oakland, CA	Diploma

CERTIFICATES

2014–Present	Certified Pharmacy Technician	Successfully Completed Pharmacy Technician Certification Board Exam

> As shown here, certification can be a separate category.

COMMUNITY SERVICE

January 2013–Present (8 Hours/Month)	Volunteer	Metropolitan Area Food Bank Oakland, CA

REFERENCES

Furnished Upon Request

Actual résumé size is 8.5 x 11 inches.

RÉSUMÉ 5 Lia Kim Chang

Two-page chronological résumé of a student seeking a pharmacy internship.
Font: Garamond 11 point.

> The objective and summary statement play up her skills.

Lia Kim Chang

1571 Camellia Drive
San Francisco, California 94122

Telephone: 415.566.8507
E-mail: chang525@aol.com

CAREER OBJECTIVE

To obtain a pharmacy internship that builds on my strengths, expands my knowledge, and allows me to contribute to the organization's goals.

PROFESSIONAL SUMMARY

Pharmacy intern with excellent interpersonal, leadership, and organizational skills. Background in research, patient education, and pharmacy practice.

EDUCATION

University of California at San Francisco — 2013–Present
School of Pharmacy — Degree anticipated May 2017
San Francisco, California

Santa Clara University — 2009–2013
Santa Clara, California — B.S. in Biology

> The way she spotlights her achievements lets readers know that she is someone who gets things done.

PROFESSIONAL EXPERIENCE

Pharmacy Technician, St. John's Medical Center — 2011–Present
San Francisco, California — (Part-time)

- Conducted in-store study with over 100 patients, comparing effectiveness of web-based tools to communicate information about drug therapy and drug interactions
- Organized and updated records from pharmacists' patient counseling sessions
- Presented information sessions for senior patients on new drug therapies and generic options for treatment
- Initiated and organized quarterly monthly "brown bag" sessions in the Medical Center's cafeteria in which pharmacists to review prescription medications of seniors

Actual résumé size is 8.5 x 11 inches.

RÉSUMÉ 5 Lia Kim Chang *(continued)*

Although many people do not use two-page résumés until they have many years of work experience, this résumé contains good information and would be too cramped on one page.

Lia Kim Chang (Page 2)

PROFESSIONAL EXPERIENCE (Continued)

Pharmacy Technician, Longs Drugs — 2009–2010
Santa Clara, California — (Summer)

- Researched and recommended support groups for patients with ongoing medication needs and medical conditions, including asthma, diabetes, allergies, and osteoporosis
- Evaluated options for updating telephone system to make requesting prescription refills easier for patients
- Collaborated with two other technicians to publicize expanded wellness programs

Laboratory Assistant I — 2007–2008
Biology Department — (Summer)
Santa Clara University

- Inventoried and reordered supplies and maintained stock records for department chair
- Mentored students in two sections of Introduction to Biology summer course

MEMBERSHIPS

American Pharmacists Association - Academy of Student Pharmacists (APhA-ASP)	2013–Present
California Pharmacists Association	2013–Present

AWARDS AND HONORS

APhA-ASP Chapter Vice President	2016
Chair, Operation Diabetes Campaign promoting early screening and detection	2015
Poster Presentation, Diabetes Awareness, APhA-ASP Region 8 Midyear Meeting, October 14–16, Las Vegas	2015
Service Award, Friend to Friend, for leading drive to supply wigs and scarves to low-income cancer patients	2014
Beta Beta Beta National Biological Honor Society	2011–2013
Dean's List, College of Arts and Sciences Santa Clara University	2010–2013

Actual résumé size is 8.5 x 11 inches.

RÉSUMÉ 6 Amanda Ashley Sanderson

This combination résumé for a pharmacy student has a particularly attractive format.
Font: Georgia 11 and 10 point.

> Résumé may have been prepared for distribution at a job fair because it lacks an objective. When you are applying for a specific opportunity, tailor your objective to match.

Amanda Ashley Sanderson
4145 Alton Lane
Denver, Colorado 80249
303.375.8019
303.237.8754 (Mobile)
amanda.sanderson@uchsc.edu
www.aasanderson.wix.com/eportfolio

EDUCATION

University of Colorado Health Sciences Center — August 2014–Present
School of Pharmacy, Denver, Colorado
Doctor of Pharmacy degree anticipated, May 2018

University of Colorado — September 2010–June 2014
Boulder, Colorado
B.A. in Biochemistry

EXPERIENCE

Pharmacy Technician — June 2014–August 2015 (Summers)
Walgreens, Denver, Colorado
Supervisor: Debra A. Ferrell, R.Ph.
Primary responsibilities: Assisted the pharmacist in preparing prescription medications for dispensing, processed insurance claims, maintained an inventory for prescription drug products, nonprescription drug products, and medical devices

Research Assistant — June 2013–August 2013
Department of Chemistry, University of Colorado at Boulder
Advisor: Joseph N. Shockley, Ph.D.
Primary responsibilities: Assisted with biochemical and biophysical studies of sensory receptors and signaling proteins

Receptionist — May 2012–August 2012
Steven V. Edmonds, M.D., Grand Junction, Colorado
Supervisor: Nancy Holmes
Primary responsibilities: Arranging appointments for patients and performing general clerical duties

> Listing supervisors is a convention seen on many pharmacy résumés. It is a plus when the supervisor is a known leader or innovator in pharmacy.

COMMUNITY SERVICE

Volunteer — June 2009–August 2009
Memorial Hospital, Grand Junction, Colorado
Primary Activities: Delivered meals to patients, participated in a diabetes screening clinic by measuring blood pressures, assisted in the coordination of a community blood drive

Actual résumé size is 8.5 x 11 inches.

RÉSUMÉ 6 Amanda Ashley Sanderson *(continued)*

AMANDA ASHLEY SANDERSON (Page 2)

CERTIFICATION AND LICENSURE

Pharmacy Intern No. 762 Colorado Board of Pharmacy	May 2017
Certificate of Occupational Proficiency in Emergency Medical Technology Colorado Mountain College Glenwood Springs, Colorado	July 2012

MEMBERSHIPS

Academy of Student Pharmacists	2014–Present
American Pharmacists Association	2014–Present
Colorado Society of Health-System Pharmacists Student Chapter	2015–Present
Ski and Snowboard Club, University of Colorado at Boulder	2011–2014

RELATED INFORMATION

A list of references is available upon request.

An electronic version of this resume will be provided upon request.

Actual résumé size is 8.5 x 11 inches.

RÉSUMÉ 7 Amanda Ashley Sanderson – Electronic Version

Electronic version of résumé 6.
Font: Tahoma 12 and 10 point.

AMANDA ASHLEY SANDERSON

ADDRESS

4145 Alton Lane
Denver, Colorado 80249
303.375.8019
303.237.8754, Cellular
amanda.sanderson@uchsc.edu
www.aasanderson.wix.com/eportfolio

EDUCATION

University of Colorado Health Sciences Center
School of Pharmacy, Denver, Colorado
August 2014–Present
Doctor of Pharmacy degree anticipated, May 2018

University of Colorado
Boulder, Colorado
September 2010–June 2014
B.A. in Biochemistry

EXPERIENCE

Pharmacy Technician
Walgreens, Denver, Colorado
Supervisor: Debra A. Ferrell, R.Ph.
June 2014–August 2015 (Summers)
Primary responsibilities: Assisted the pharmacist in preparing prescription medications for dispensing, processed insurance claims, maintained an inventory for prescription drug products, non-prescription drug products, and medical devices

Research Assistant
Department of Chemistry, University of Colorado at Boulder
Advisor: Joseph N. Shockley, Ph.D.
June 2013–August 2013
Primary responsibilities: Assisted with biochemical and biophysical studies of sensory receptors and signaling proteins

Receptionist
Steven V. Edmonds, M.D., Grand Junction, Colorado
Supervisor: Nancy Holmes
May 2012–August 2012
Primary responsibilities: Arranging appointments for patients and performing general clerical duties

Actual résumé size is 8.5 x 11 inches.

RÉSUMÉ 7 Amanda Ashley Sanderson – Electronic Version *(continued)*

AMANDA ASHLEY SANDERSON, Page 2

COMMUNITY SERVICE

Volunteer
Memorial Hospital, Grand Junction, Colorado
June 2009–August 2009
Primary Activities: Delivered meals to patients, participated in a diabetes screening clinic by measuring blood pressures, assisted in the coordination of a community blood drive

CERTIFICATION AND LICENSURE

Pharmacy Intern No. 762
Colorado Board of Pharmacy
Expires July 2018

Certificate of Occupational Proficiency
in Emergency Medical Technology
Colorado Mountain College
Glenwood Springs, Colorado
Expires December 2018

MEMBERSHIPS

American Pharmacists Association
Academy of Student Pharmacists
2014–Present

Colorado Society of Health-System Pharmacists
Student Chapter, 2015–Present

Ski and Snowboard Club, University of Colorado
at Boulder, 2011–2014

RELATED INFORMATION

A list of references is available upon request.

A properly formatted hard copy of this electronic resume will be provided upon request.

Actual résumé size is 8.5 x 11 inches.

RÉSUMÉ 8 Ronald James Harrison

A chronological résumé for a graduating pharmacy student.
Font: Verdana 11 point.

Ronald James Harrison

2910 Roswell Terrace	Atlanta, Georgia 30303 rjharris@peachnet.com	(404) 220-5001

Objective To seek a community pharmacy practice residency

Education

Mercer University Southern School of Pharmacy Atlanta, Georgia	2013–Present Pharm.D. Candidate, 2017 Cumulative G.P.A.: 3.4 /4.0
Macon State College Macon, Georgia	2009–2013 Pre-Pharmacy Curriculum

Experience

Pharmacy Intern CVS Pharmacy Atlanta, Georgia	October 2014-Present
Emergency Room Technician Medical Center of Central Georgia Macon, Georgia	June 2012–August 2013 (Part-time)

Licenses

Georgia Board of Pharmacy Internship License # 1059	April 2013

Concise and easy to skim, this résumé gives the most essential data. It could expand on the candidate's achievements and leadership experience.

Awards and Recognition

Phi Lambda Sigma	2015–Present
School of Pharmacy Dean's List	Fall Semesters, 2014 and 2015
A.T. Simpson Scholarship Award	2014

Professional Affiliations

Student National Pharmaceutical Association — 2013–Present
- President, 2011–2012
- Treasurer, 2010–2011

Academy of Student Pharmacists (ASP), American Pharmacists Association — 2013–Present
- 2013 Delegate, ASP Annual Convention

References

References and additional information provided upon request

Actual résumé size is 8.5 x 11 inches.

RÉSUMÉ 9 Kenneth R. Crow

Résumé of a pharmacist who has completed residency training.
Font: Lucida Sans 11 point.

An objective, although not essential, would help readers understand what sort of position he is looking for.

Kenneth R. Crow
2331 Marsh Street
Oklahoma City, Oklahoma 73159
(405) 688-2091
Kenneth.Crow@med.va.gov

Education

Doctor of Pharmacy
2011–2015
University of Texas
San Antonio, Texas

Bachelor of Science in Pharmacy
2009–2011
University of Oklahoma
Oklahoma City, Oklahoma

Pre-Pharmacy Curriculum
2007–2009
University of Oklahoma
Norman, Oklahoma

Professional Training

Specialized Residency in Primary Care Pharmacy Practice
2016–2017
University of Oklahoma College of Pharmacy and Veterans Affairs Medical Center

Residency in Pharmacy Practice
2015–2016
Integris Baptist Medical Center
Oklahoma City, Oklahoma

Licenses and Certificates

Pharmacist No. 3065 (2015) — Texas State Board of Pharmacy
Pharmacist No. 1764 (2015) — Oklahoma State Board of Pharmacy
Advanced Cardiac Life Support Provider (2014) — American Heart Association

Awards and Honors–University of Oklahoma

Rho Chi, Gamma Chapter, 2013
Phi Lambda Sigma, Alpha Epsilon, 2014
Dean's List, 2009–2011

This bare bones list is easy to skim, but it fails to highlight unique experiences and achievements that set this candidate apart from others.

Actual résumé size is 8.5 x 11 inches.

RÉSUMÉ 9 Kenneth R. Crow (*continued*)

Kenneth R. Crow, Page 2

Current Professional Memberships

Oklahoma Society of Health-System Pharmacists
American Society of Health-System Pharmacists
American Pharmacists Association
American College of Clinical Pharmacy

This résumé could be shortened to one page without sacrificing readability by reducing the spacing between sections. Recruiters tend to prefer one-page résumés.

References

Available Upon Request

Actual résumé size is 8.5 x 11 inches.

RÉSUMÉ 10 Kirit Raman Patel

This two-page chronological résumé shows a variety of professional experience.
Font: Century Schoolbook 11 and 10 point.

Summary gives readers a preview of information in the body of the résumé.

Kirit Raman Patel

9086 Haywood Street
Philadelphia, Pennsylvania 19120

Telephone ▪ (215) 276-2492
Telepage ▪ (215) 582-8067
E-mail ▪ krpatel@mindspring.com

Summary Newly licensed pharmacist with experience providing highly skilled services in community and hospital pharmacies and in manufacturing. Demonstrated leadership and communication through organizing and delivering community health campaigns, patient education, and staff presentations.

Education

2010–2016 University of the Sciences in Philadelphia — Doctor of Pharmacy degree awarded
Philadelphia College of Pharmacy
Philadelphia, Pennsylvania

Professional Experience and Achievements

Useful details are provided here.

Summers 2014 and 2015 — GlaxoSmithKline — Quality Control Technician
Philadelphia, Pennsylvania
Ensured compliance with rigorous quality standards through inspection and statistical sampling. Audited productivity statistics from peers during mandatory review cycles. Prepared and gave staff presentations on quality control advances.

Summer 2013 — Rite Aid Pharmacy — Pharmacy Intern
Philadelphia, Pennsylvania
Assisted two pharmacists in filling more than 2000 prescriptions per week. Reduced inventory carrying costs by 10% by conscientiously controlling prescription drug inventory.

Summer 2012 — St. Luke's Hospital — Pharmacy Intern
Harrisburg, Pennsylvania
Managed medication counseling center for low-income patients. Wrote and designed patient checklists and information sheets. Scheduled pharmacists and physicians for counseling sessions. Maintained records for patients and reviewed recommendations for potential medication interactions.

Summer 2011 — Rite Aid Pharmacy — Pharmacy Intern
Harrisburg, Pennsylvania
Assisted in routine prescription processing. Processed prescription insurance claims. Developed fact sheet and flyer for blood pressure screenings.

2008–2010 (Part-time) — Mitchell's Apothecary — Clerk
Harrisburg, Pennsylvania
Interacted with clients, responded to inquiries, placed orders for supplies, helped maintain records and files.

Actual résumé size is 8.5 x 11 inches.

RÉSUMÉ 10 Kirit Raman Patel *(continued)*

Kirit Raman Patel **Page 2**

Licenses

2011	Pennsylvania State Board of Pharmacy	Intern
2016	Pennsylvania State Board of Pharmacy	Pharmacist

Recognition and Awards

University of the Sciences in Philadelphia

- 2016 — Community Service Award
- 2015 — William P. Johnson Scholarship
- 2015 — Patient Counseling Competition Winner
- 2014 — Rho Chi Academic Honor Society, Alpha Tau Chapter
- 2013 — Dr. James R. Mitchell Scholarship

GlaxoSmithKline

- 2014 — Employee of the Month, Quality Control Section

Memberships

2015–2016 Student Government Association, University of the Sciences
- Vice-President of Activities

2014–Present Pennsylvania Society of Health-System Pharmacists
- Member, Legislative Affairs Committee (2013–2014)

2013–Present Phi Delta Chi Fraternity

2012–Present American Pharmacists Association - Academy of Student Pharmacists (APhA-ASP)
- Coordinator, Professional Projects (2014–2015)
- Treasurer (2008–2009)
- Member, Legislative Affairs Committee (2012–2013)

2012–Present Pennsylvania Society of Health-System Pharmacists
- Member, Legislative Affairs Committee (2013–2014)

Computer Skills

Software Proficiency
- Microsoft Office

Desktop Publishing
- JAVA Script
- Hypertext Markup Language

Service Activities

American Pharmacists Association - Academy of Student Pharmacists (APhA-ASP)

- 2015 — Diabetes Screening Campaign Chairman
- 2015 — "Flu Shot" Campaign Committee Member
- 2014 — Blood Pressure Screening Coordinator
- 2013 — Alzheimer's Association Memory Walk, Participant
- 2012 — Blood Pressure Screening Committee Member

Phi Delta Chi Professional Pharmacy Fraternity

- 2015 — Thanksgiving Food Drive Coordinator

Actual résumé size is 8.5 x 11 inches.

RÉSUMÉ 11 Gina Maria Ruiz

A functional or skills résumé for a home infusion pharmacist, formerly a nurse.
Font: Arial 12 point.

Gina Maria Ruiz
6105 Fulton Way, Lubbock, Texas 79410 (806) 795-6212

CAREER PROFILE

- Twenty years of experience with health care education and practice
- Twelve years' experience as a practicing registered pharmacist
- Two years' experience as a practicing registered nurse
- Excellent interpersonal communication and team-building skills

Career profile encapsulates key details.

HIGHLIGHTS OF PROFESSIONAL EXPERIENCE

Pharmacy Practice

- Staff experience in both community and hospital practice settings
- Management experience in a home infusion pharmacy practice
- Teaching experience as a preceptor for pharmacy interns and clerkship students
- Managed The Joint Commission accreditation process for a home infusion therapy service
- Certified diabetic educator

Nursing Practice

- Staff experience in both ambulatory care and inpatient settings
- Teaching experience in a prenatal care clinic

EMPLOYMENT HISTORY

Johnson's Pharmacy and Home Infusion Services, Abilene, Texas

- Director of Pharmacy, Home Infusion Services, 2011–Present
- Pharmacist-in-Charge, 2009–2011
- Staff Pharmacist, 2005–2009

St. Vincent's Hospital, Abilene, Texas

- Staff Nurse, 1994–1996

Professional experience listed above directs employers' attention to strengths and away from employment gaps.

EDUCATION

University of Houston College of Pharmacy, Houston, Texas
Bachelor of Science in Pharmacy, degree conferred 1999

Hardin-Simmons University, Abilene, Texas
Pre-Pharmacy Curriculum, 2000–2002

St. Vincent's Hospital School of Nursing, Abilene, Texas
Diploma in Nursing, awarded 1994

Actual résumé size is 8.5 x 11 inches.

RÉSUMÉ 12 Valerie Nga Tran

Résumé of someone in academia. This person most likely uses a CV more often than a résumé, but it is good to have both.
Font: Times New Roman 12 point.

A summary or objective would help readers understand her specific strengths and what position she is looking for.

Valerie Nga Tran

CONTACT INFORMATION

University Address:	Department of Pharmaceutical Sciences The University of Connecticut School of Pharmacy, U-84 Storrs, Connecticut 06269-8320 Phone: 860-486-3285 E-mail: vnt97003@uconnvm.uconn.edu
Home Address:	2313 Wildwood Way Storrs, Connecticut 06268 Phone: 860-429-6679 E-mail: vntran5@hotmail.com

EDUCATION

University of Connecticut School of Pharmacy Storrs, Connecticut	Ph.D. in Pharmaceutical Sciences Pharmaceutics Concentration August 2013–Present Degree anticipated, May 2017 Major Advisor: Harold J. Lee, Ph.D.
Rutgers University College of Pharmacy Piscataway, New Jersey	B.S. in Pharmacy with Distinction Degree conferred, May 2013

TEACHING EXPERIENCE

Graduate Teaching Assistant	Pharmacy 209 (Physicochemical Principles of Drugs, 1 Semester Hour, Laboratory, Fall Semesters, 2014–2016)
Lecturer and Tutor	Pharmacy 208 and 210 (Physicochemical Principles of Drugs I and II, 3 Semester Hours, Fall and Spring Semesters, 2014–2016)

RESEARCH EXPERIENCE

M.S. Thesis	The Effects of Temperature and Moisture on the Stability of Freeze-Dried Prostaglandin E1
Ph.D. Thesis	Diode Laser Induced Fluorescence Detection of Daunorubicin in Plasma Using Pressurized Electrochromatography

Actual résumé size is 8.5 x 11 inches.

RÉSUMÉ 12 Valerie Nga Tran *(continued)*

Valerie Nga Tran **Page 2**

SELECTED PUBLICATIONS

Tran VN, Lee HJ, Freisen TY. The effects of temperature and moisture on the stability of freeze dried prostaglandin E1. *Biopharm Drug Dispos* 2008;23:213–217.

Tran VN, Watson FN, Tyler AB, Lee HJ. Diode laser induced fluoresence detection of daunorubicin in plasma. *J Pharm Sci* 2011; In press.

The facts of her background are listed in a clear, concise way.

AFFILIATIONS

2012–Present	American Pharmacists Association
2013–Present	Connecticut Pharmacists Association
2014–Present	Student Chapter of the American Association of Pharmaceutical Scientists

AWARDS AND HONORS

2015	Pre-Doctoral Fellowship, American Foundation for Pharmaceutical Education
2012	S.W. Higgins Scholarship Award, Rutgers University College of Pharmacy
2011	Rho Chi Society, Alpha Eta Chapter, Rutgers University
2011	Who's Who Among Students in American Universities and Colleges
2008–2013	Dean's List, Rutgers University College of Pharmacy (All semesters)

REFERENCES

Available upon request

Actual résumé size is 8.5 x 11 inches.

RÉSUMÉ 13 Eduardo Antonio Foster

Résumé of a pharmacist/attorney working in the pharmaceutical industry.
Font: Arial 12 point.

Eduardo Antonio Foster

Department of Regulatory Affairs
PharmaMedica, Inc.
3 Langford Parkway
Wallingford, CT 06492
(203) 564-7820
fosterea@pm.com

942 Derbyshire Court
Middletown, Connecticut 06457
(860) 447-6720
fosterea@execulink.net

PROFESSIONAL SUMMARY

Licensed pharmacist/attorney with 20 years' experience in drug regulation, budget administration, department and project management, and service delivery. Extensive leadership in presentation, interpersonal, and team-building skills. Established track record of meeting and exceeding established goals related to management, training, and education. Bilingual, Spanish and English.

Summary highlights his unique attributes.

EDUCATION

Juris Doctor, University of Arizona, Tucson 2000–2003
B.S. in Pharmacy, University of Arizona, Tucson 1992–1997

PROFESSIONAL EXPERIENCE

Director of Regulatory Affairs 2012–Present
PharmaMedica, Inc., Wallingford, CT

- Spearhead development and implementation of regulatory policies and procedures for licensure of Respitoria®
- Review and execute over 10 investigational drug applications, new drug applications, and abbreviated new drug applications yearly
- Interpret and apply all regulations and guidelines of the Food and Drug Administration concerning drug development
- Prepare and implement annual strategic plan for department of over 75 employees
- Allocate and coordinate departmental resources

Clinical Science Manager 2007–2012
Invion Biologicals, San Francisco, CA

- Enhanced client relations as liaison for communicating medical and scientific data
- Led and facilitated biweekly workflow planning and review seminars
- Organized monthly multidisciplinary work sessions to develop cross-functional team expertise
- Screened and updated drug development and clinical research procedures weekly
- Maintained open and positive communications with regulatory authorities

Actual résumé size is 8.5 x 11 inches.

RÉSUMÉ 13 Eduardo Antonio Foster *(continued)*

The way he uses numbers to emphasize responsibilities and achievements is effective.

Eduardo Antonio Foster **Page 2**

PROFESSIONAL EXPERIENCE (Continued)

Clinical Research Associate II 2003–2007
Stratton Pharmaceuticals, La Jolla, CA

- Coordinated and supervised initiation, execution, and analysis of clinical studies of three investigational drugs
- Mentored and supervised 18 Clinical Research Assistants
- Evaluated and selected over 15 Contract Research Organizations yearly
- Arranged and conducted monthly investigator meetings
- Researched and strengthened knowledge in clinical areas of diabetes and infectious disease

Pharmacist (Part-time) 2000–2002
Thompson Apothecary, Scottsdale, AZ

- Received and assessed written prescriptions from over 200 prescribers monthly
- Maintained over 500 patient profiles detailing prescription and nonprescription medications and major health conditions
- Delivered and interpreted drug information to prescribers and patients

Pharmaceutical Sales Representative 1997–2003
J.H. Downing Company, Phoenix, AZ

Accomplished over 100 calls per month to practicing physicians, pharmacists, hospitals, and other health-related organizations
Provided information about 24 drug products marketed by J.H. Downing Company
Completed two-year training in sales strategies and skills

PROFESSIONAL CREDENTIALS

State Bar of Arizona, Admission 2003
Arizona Board of Pharmacy, License 8875 1997

PROFESSIONAL AND COMMUNITY AFFILIATIONS

American Society for Pharmacy Law 2010–Present
Rotary International Service Organization 2007–Present
Arizona Pharmacy Association 1994–Present
American Pharmacists Association 1994–Present

AWARDS AND RECOGNITION

Community Service Achievement Award 2012
Invion Biologicals

Rotary Volunteers Certificate of Recognition 2011
San Francisco-area Rotary Club

Actual résumé size is 8.5 x 11 inches.

RÉSUMÉ 14 Gerald Gregory Schmidt

Résumé of a pharmacist practicing in a large corporation.
Font: Century Gothic 11 point.

Gerald Gregory Schmidt

4085 Miami Lakes Drive
Hialeah, Florida 33014

(305) 620-8642
ggs007@yahoo.com

EDUCATION

1997–2000	University of Florida College of Pharmacy Gainesville, Florida Bachelor of Science degree in Pharmacy
1994–1997	Stetson University DeLand, Florida Pre-pharmacy curriculum

This space could be better used to highlight skills and achievements rather than listing each location. Résumé is very sketchy.

EMPLOYMENT

2014–Present	Pharmacist, Walgreens Company • 830 Miami Lakes Drive, Hialeah, Florida
2000–2014	Pharmacist, CVS • 15585 Miami Lakes Drive, Hialeah, Florida • 8842 Golden Gate Parkway, Naples, Florida • 1868 Immokalee Road, Naples, Florida • 2635 Tamiami Trail, Port Charlotte, Florida • 8335 West Water Avenue, Tampa, Florida • 6220 North Florida Avenue, Tampa, Florida

LICENSURE

2000–Present	Pharmacist (License # PS20376, June 30, 1994) Florida Board of Pharmacy

PROFESSIONAL MEMBERSHIPS

2000–Present	Florida Pharmacy Association
2000–Present	American Pharmacists Association

REFERENCES

Available upon request

Actual résumé size is 8.5 x 11 inches.

RÉSUMÉ 15 Mark Alan Chandler

Chronological résumé of a health-system pharmacist.
Font: Times New Roman 11 point.

Summary is helpful, but its content is not fully backed up by the descriptions of his experience below.

Mark Alan Chandler

Professional Summary

Hospital pharmacist with more than 25 years' experience, primarily in VA system, and instructor of technicians and pharmacy and nursing students. Broad experience addressing medication needs of hospitalized patients, including preparing IV and unit dose medications, drug information, drug interaction monitoring, nutritional services, antibiotic dosing and selection, and inventory management. Experience with EPIC system.

Contact Information

Home:	25816 Park Hills Ave, South Holland, Illinois 60615 (708) 368-4219; chand282@excite.com
Work:	Pharmacy Service (119), Edward Hines Jr. VA Hospital 5th Avenue and Roosevelt Road, Hines, Illinois 60141 (708) 202-1872; machan@mail.va.gov

Education

1982–1987	Purdue University College of Pharmacy West Lafayette, Indiana Bachelor of Science Degree, Pharmacy

Work Experience

1998–Present	Edward Hines Jr. VA Hospital, Hines, Illinois Pharmacist, Pharmacy Service
1994–1998	Spokane VA Medical Center, Spokane, Washington Pharmacist, Pharmacy Service
1987–1994	Mount Carmel Hospital, Columbus, Ohio Pharmacist, Department of Pharmacy Services

Teaching Experience

2010–Present	South Suburban College, South Holland, Illinois Instructor, Pharmacy Technician Program
1994–1998	Washington State University College of Pharmacy Pullman, Washington Instructor, Pharmacy Externship Program
1992–1994	Mount Carmel Hospital School of Nursing Columbus, Ohio Instructor, Pharmacology and Nursing Calculations

Professional Affiliations

2001–Present	Illinois Council of Health-System Pharmacists ▪ Treasurer, 2014–Present ▪ Organizational Affairs Committee, 2009–2014
1992–Present	American Society of Health-System Pharmacists
1987–Present	Purdue Pharmacy Alumni Association

Actual résumé size is 8.5 x 11 inches.

Preparing Your Curriculum Vitae

CHAPTER 6

A curriculum vitae, or CV, outlines your personal background, education, and experience. Unlike a résumé, a CV provides more comprehensive information and usually exceeds one or two pages. Many health professionals, academics, and people in other specialized professions, such as law and engineering, prefer CVs, because they contain additional detail about qualifications and activities.

In the pharmacy field, CVs routinely accompany applications for admission to graduate and professional degree programs, employment, internships, postgraduate residencies, fellowships, consulting positions, and organizational leadership positions, as well as grant proposals and nominations for honors and awards.

In contrast, a résumé briefly summarizes the same information and is used primarily when you apply for a specific employment opportunity. When potential employers expect a large applicant pool, they prefer résumés: they can skim them more quickly. Most health professionals prepare both a résumé and CV, because they accommodate differing needs.

Never Say "Curriculum Vita"

"Curriculum vitae" is a Latin term that means "course of life." When used in conjunction with "curriculum," the word "vitae" (a genitive singular feminine noun), not "vita," is the correct choice. If you say or write "curriculum vita," it is incorrect. However, you can use only the term "vita," because it refers to a document that contains information about one's personal, educational, and experience qualifications.

Source: Adapted from Becker AS. Personal communication concerning the use of Latin terms. Blacksburg, VA: Virginia Polytechnic Institute and State University; August 21, 2000.

Preparing the Curriculum Vitae

The process of preparing the CV involves the identical principle used for a résumé: presenting your education, experience, and accomplishments clearly and concisely. Because you do not need to restrict the document's length, however, you can provide more complete information and include additional category headings. The sidebar contains a list of typical categories found on a CV.

Because a CV should highlight your strengths, you can include any number of other categories, such as leadership experience, military background, special skills, or consulting

Typical Information Categories on CVs

The following list presents the categories of information generally provided on the CVs of pharmacy professionals:

- Personal information
- Educational background
- Postgraduate training
- Professional practice experience
- Other work experience
- Licensure and certification
- Research experience
- Teaching experience
- Publications
- Presentations
- Professional memberships
- Service activities
- Awards and honors
- References

experience. The order of the sections and the actual titles you give them will vary on an individual basis. Traditionally, pharmacy professionals place their education before their professional experience.

Personal Information

A CV usually begins with "Curriculum Vitae" placed at the top of the first page, followed by your full legal name or first name, middle initial, and last name. Next, list personal information such as a temporary and permanent address, telephone number, and e-mail address. You can present this information directly under your name or organize it under a heading such as "personal information" or "contact information."

As explained in Chapter 4, many people include personal information on their CV that they do not put on their résumé. However, you do not need to provide any personal details other than your contact information. For example, why include your date of birth? Age is not relevant for a position unless specifically stated. Likewise, omit your Social Security number, nationality, marital status, and a statement about health. Do not include a photograph with your CV unless one has been requested for a specific purpose. If asked to supply a photograph, use a passport-sized head shot.

Career Objective

As a general rule, most pharmacists and health professionals do not put a career objective on their CV. You may want to include one, however, depending on how you intend to use the CV. For example, prospective employers who request your CV may appreciate seeing a career objective to get a sense of the type of position you are seeking. Sometimes, including a career objective can help highlight special knowledge and skills that you want to call to your reader's immediate attention.

Educational Experience

List your educational experience in reverse chronological order, and include the name and location of the institution, dates of attendance, and the type of degree earned. If you did not complete a degree, you can still add a major or area of study, with or without the number of credit hours earned. If you took only one or two courses at an institution to fulfill a degree requirement, you do not need to include them. Also, you should not include high school credentials if you have a college degree or have earned at least two years of college credits.

You can present your academic standing as a cumulative grade point average, class ranking, or graduation honor (e.g., graduated magna cum laude). Most people consider it optional to include academic standing, but if you earned exceptional grades, you may want to highlight them. If you apply for a residency, fellowship, or graduate position, you should always include your academic standing.

Professional Training

If you have completed a residency or fellowship, earned certification as a technician, or received other professional training, you can list it in the education section, include it in the professional experience section, or create a separate section. It is your choice. If you consider your professional training an important extension of the educational process, for example, you may want to combine it with your educational background.

On the other hand, you may want to give professional training a separate heading if you do not want to overshadow your academic credentials and would like to call special attention to your internship or residency. Or you may decide it fits best within the professional practice experience section, especially if the training was recent. In this case, it will stand out by falling at the top of your reverse chronological listing.

When listing professional training, make sure to include the name and location of the institution where you received your specialized training, dates of attendance, and the type of certificate or credential earned.

Professional Experience

The professional experience section deserves prominence on the CV. Ideally, you should devote this section to your experience within the profession. Do not include other, less relevant work here; instead, include it elsewhere on your CV.

People at the beginning of their careers, however, may want to combine professional and other work experiences under a single heading such as "employment experience." Those with extensive professional experience may wish to leave out other work experience altogether, unless their history involves more than one established career.

You can include volunteer experience in this section if your commitment was sustained over time and required you to apply professional knowledge and skills. The experience gained through volunteerism, especially in a health care–related activity, provides as much value as that acquired through a paid position. You can also consider placing this type of information in a section devoted to "public service," "community service," or "service activities."

When preparing your "professional experience" listings, include the following:

- Name and location of the employer or volunteer agency
- Beginning and ending dates of employment
- Title of the position held
- A description of duties

When describing each position, use action verbs to emphasize your accomplishments. (See Table 4.2 for many common action verbs used in pharmacy-related résumés and CVs.) Keep descriptions brief and organize key information as lists preceded by bullets or dashes. You do not need to give the supervisor's name and contact information for each position, especially if you have included one or more of these names in your reference list.

Licensure and Certification

Document the types of licenses and certificates you hold, as well as their status. Include the awarding agency, license number, date of issue, and most recent renewal date.

List certificates acknowledging the successful completion of training programs chronologically, with the most recent certificate listed first. State the full title of the certificate, the organization awarding it, and the date of certification. Examples of applicable certificates include a pharmacy technician training program, a residency training program, a cardiopulmonary resuscitation training program, or a Board of Pharmacy Specialties examination.

Research Experience

In this section, you can showcase all research and scholarly pursuits, including grants, contracts, patents, and projects. List them in reverse chronological order, and include the title, sponsoring agency or corporation, requested funding, date of submission, and outcome of the submission. In general, these listings should not include a description of the work.

If you are a student, include the title of your research or scholarly activity, name of the institution, names of coinvestigators such as a major professor or other faculty, and dates of the activity. You can also briefly describe the special knowledge or skills you acquired.

Teaching Experience

Many health professionals include teaching experience and faculty appointments on their CVs. Although you can place this information in the professional experience section, it achieves greater prominence if you create a special section. For each appointment or activity, list the institution, course number and title, date provided, and the number of students involved. Examples of teaching experience to list on your CV include the following:

- Lecturing (consider specifying the type and size of group)
- Coordinating conferences
- Conducting workshops or recitation sessions
- Serving as a mentor
- Precepting students in a practice environment
- Providing continuing education to practitioners
- Preparing electronic course materials

Publications

Publications you can list on your CV include articles you have published in professional journals, books you have authored, and reports you have prepared. You can also include scholarly work in nontraditional media such as electronic software packages or audiovisual productions. You may choose to highlight your name in a citation, especially if the citation includes multiple authors.

For guidelines on how to cite publications properly, check standard reference guides such as *The Chicago Manual of Style* or the *American Medical Association Manual of Style.* Following a uniform style ensures that the order of each element (author, title of publication, date), as well as the way you use punctuation, italics, and other features, stays consistent for each publication you list.

Presentations

Presentations, especially invited presentations, reflect your professional experience and scholarship. They show prospective employers that you are knowledgeable, articulate, and a respected person in your field. List your presentations in reverse chronological order and provide the title of each, as well as the inviting or sponsoring organization, location, and date.

Awards and Honors

Whether you decide to announce your awards, honors, and other recognition near the beginning or end of your CV remains your preference. Because not everyone reads a CV through to the end, you may want to highlight a particularly impressive honor near the beginning. On the other hand, positioning a lengthy list of accolades near the end of the CV leaves room at the beginning for other key material. Use your judgment, but wherever you place awards and

Tip: If you participate extensively in professional organizations, consider creating a separate section on your CV titled "leadership experience." Adding this section allows you to highlight specific offices you have held in various organizations and to elaborate a bit on your leadership role.

honors, use reverse chronological order. Include the name of the award, sponsoring organization, location where given, and date.

Professional Memberships

You can document membership in professional organizations or associations in a section titled "professional memberships" or "membership in organizations." Provide the name of the organization and dates of membership (represented as "1994–Present" or "1994–2005"). In this section you can also highlight offices you have held or note other kinds of participation, such as committee memberships or task force assignments.

Service Activities

A section on service activities can document professional or personal efforts to meet the needs of the profession or community. Service to the profession, for example, might involve holding an office in an organization or serving on a university committee. Your listing of activities will reflect your own definition of service.

Make sure that you do not include items more than once in the CV's body. For example, if you list your volunteer activities in the professional experience section, do not repeat them in the service activities section.

References

The final item on your CV relates to references. As with résumés, do not list references on the CV. Create a separate page that provides the name of each reference along with complete contact information, including mailing address, telephone number, fax number, and e-mail address. If desired, you can also include a brief statement about what each reference can contribute concerning your knowledge, skills, and abilities. Although some people send their reference page along with their CV, hold off until a prospective employer specifically requests your reference list.

Other Sections

Depending on your individual experience and attributes, you may want to include other sections. "Military service," for example, would note your branch of service, entry and discharge dates, rank, type of discharge, and reserves activity. Military service is usually listed in reverse chronological order according to rank.

Your CV's Appearance

Just like résumés, CVs should be neat, appeal to the reader's eye, and adhere to basic guidelines for readability. If potential employers find your CV difficult to read, they may not bother. Also, proofread your CV carefully for typographical and mechanical errors. Make sure that each page carries your full name as well as a page number in case pieces of the CV become separated. Print a copy to proofread, check for spacing inconsistencies, and check for excessive white space on each page.

Once you have developed a standard version of your CV, consider preparing versions suitable for scanning and electronic transmission. Chapter 4 provides guidelines for creating scannable and electronic documents.

CHAPTER 7

Tips, Checklists, and Sample Curricula Vitae

Tip: Place your highest-priority categories toward the beginning of your CV so readers see them easily.

In this chapter you will find samples of curricula vitae (CV) that have various headings, formats, and content. These samples present elements that you can pick and choose to create an individualized CV. Keep in mind that the guidelines provided in Chapter 4 for organizing and preparing a résumé apply equally to a CV. As you finalize your CV, refer to the sidebar "Final Checklist of CV Elements" on page 57 to ensure you have not overlooked anything.

Design Tips

Just as with résumés, good readability and a clean appearance are crucial to successful CVs. The sidebar lists specific CV design tips.

Electronic Formats

The content of your CV will probably remain the same whether you prepare a standard, scannable, or electronic document. When preparing the latter two types, however, you may want to include specific key words in case the employer uses computer software to search your CV electronically. (See Table 4.4 for a list of common keywords for pharmacy-related electronic résumés and CVs.)

Final Evaluation

After you have prepared what you consider the final form of your CV, put it aside for a few days so you can look at it again with fresh eyes. Then go through it carefully one more time. Make sure you check for the following:

- Accuracy of details. Are all your dates, titles, and other facts correct?
- Redundancy. Have you repeated the same information in more than one place?
- Visual appeal. Is the spacing and justification consistent?

As a final "quality control" measure, ask peers and mentors to critique your CV. Remember, the order of the sections in your CV may vary depending on personal preference. Also, check your CV against the final checklist.

Design Tips for CVs

- Because CVs contain so many category headings, make them stand out by using boldface, capitalized letters, italics, or underlining.
- Choose a consistent serif font (e.g., Bookman Old Style, Courier, Georgia, Times New Roman) or a sans serif font (e.g., Arial, Lucida Sans, Tahoma, Verdana).
- Use a font size between 10 and 14 points.
- Use various design formats (e.g., bullets, lines, italics, boldface type, shading) to create a unique appearance, but do not overuse them.
- Maintain one-inch margins at the top, bottom, and sides of the document.
- Justify the left margin.
- Avoid using graphics.

Checklist for Electronic and Scannable CVs

This checklist provides a summary of the most important points for preparing a CV for transmission over the internet and storage in computer databases.

- Choose a consistent font, preferably a sans serif font such as Arial, Lucida Sans, Tahoma, or Verdana. Keep your font size between 12 and 14 points.
- Minimize the use of design elements (e.g., bullets, lines, underlining, italics, boldface type, brackets, parentheses, shading).
- Avoid the use of tabs. Instead, create spaces using the spacebar.
- Use hard carriage returns at the end of each line.
- Do not use word wrapping.
- Include common keywords related to skills likely to be included in a computer search strategy.
- Check for spelling errors before saving as a text file.
- Use capital letters for headings as a replacement for boldface type or underlining.
- Maintain one-inch margins at the top, bottom, and sides of the document.
- Justify the left margin.
- For a scannable CV, save the final document as a "text only" or "rich text format" file. Once you have printed it on paper, do not fold or staple it.
- For an electronically transmitted CV, save the final document in a suitable format (e.g., HTML for internet posting, ASCII or PDF for attaching to e-mails).

Checklist for Preparing a CV

- Use the present tense for current duties and activities; use the past tense for previous such responsibilities.
- Write out numbers between one and nine and use numerals for 10 and above.
- Use a consistent format for telephone numbers and dates.
- If abbreviating the names of states, use the proper two-letter abbreviations
- Achieve a reasonable balance between typed copy and white space so the material does not look overcrowded.
- Proofread your document carefully for grammar, spelling, syntax, and punctuation errors, and do not forget to use your computer's "spell check" feature.
- Use only one side of each page for printing.

Curricula Vitae Samples

Examples of CVs for pharmacy professionals are provided to aid readers in developing CVs that showcase their accomplishments. The approaches in the samples vary and none is perfect for everyone. Review the formats, consider the comments on each one, and develop a CV that works for your needs.

Final Checklist of CV Elements

☐ Heading

- The words "Curriculum Vitae" usually suffice.
- Full legal name or first name, middle initial, and last name.

☐ Contact Information

- Current address, telephone number (day and evening), and e-mail address.
- Permanent address, telephone number, and e-mail address (if applicable).

☐ Date the CV Was Prepared

☐ Career Objective (optional)

- Do not make your objective too vague or too specific. Make sure the objective coincides with the specific position of interest.

☐ Education

- Name of each institution and location (i.e., city and state).
- Degree or degrees earned and year.
- List residency or fellowship training with year and name of institution and location, if not included as professional experience or under a separate heading.

☐ Experience

- List positions in reverse chronological order.
- Include accurate position titles.
- List position responsibilities in brief narrative form.
- Describe skills using action-oriented phrases.
- Quantify your accomplishments when applicable.

☐ Licenses and Certificates

- Consider listing licenses and certificates with dates, if not listed in the professional experience section.

☐ Research Experience

- List grants, contracts, patents, and projects in reverse chronological order with the title, sponsoring agency or corporation, funding requested, date of submission, and outcome of the submission.
- For students, list the title of the research or scholarly activity, name of the institution, names of coinvestigators such as a major professor or other faculty, and the dates of the activity.
- For students, consider including a brief description of special knowledge or skills acquired with any research or scholarly activity.

☐ Teaching Experience

- In reverse chronological order, list the type of teaching, such as lecturing, or coordinating conference, workshop, or recitation sessions; serving as a mentor; precepting students in a practice environment; providing continuing education to practitioners; or preparing electronic course materials. Start with the name of the institution, followed by course number and title, date provided, and the number of students involved.

☐ Publications

- List all articles, monographs, books, and other publications in reverse chronological order according to the format established for biomedical journals. For guidelines, check style guides such as *The Chicago Manual of Style* or the *American Medical Association Manual of Style.*
- List nontraditional publications such as electronic software packages or audio-visual productions according to the format established for biomedical journals.

☐ Presentations

- List the title, inviting or sponsoring organization, location, and date of each presentation in reverse chronological order.

☐ Awards, Honors, and Recognition

- Identify the title, sponsor, and date of significant recognition or awards.

☐ Professional Memberships

- List the organization and inclusive dates of membership.
- List any offices held or other evidence of participation.
- If you have an extensive list of memberships, consider a separate heading such as "leadership experience" to document achievements.

☐ Service Activities

- List activity, organization, city, state, and dates.
- Consider a brief description of the activity if the title is not intuitive.
- Consider organizing entries by categories of service (e.g., profession, university, patient, community).

☐ References

- Prepare a separate page and provide the name of each reference along with complete contact information including address, telephone number, fax number, and e-mail address.
- Consider preparing a brief statement about what each reference can contribute concerning your knowledge, skills, and abilities.

CV 1 Ryan David Freeman, Page 1 of 5

A clean, straightforward, "no frills" CV for a health-system pharmacist who completed a one-year residency and has three years of experience in his current position.
Font: Times New Roman 12 point.

Curriculum Vitae

Ryan David Freeman

Boise VA Medical Center
100 Medical Center Drive
Boise, Idaho 83706
Telephone: (208) 757-0935
Facsimile: (208) 659-1840
E-mail: ryan.freeman@.boiseva.gov

2501 Nickerson Court
Boise, Idaho 83702
Telephone: (208) 225-8562
E-mail: rdfree@greatnet.com
Web: rdfreeman.weebly.com

CAREER GOAL

To seek a pharmacist supervisor position in a health-system pharmacy

EDUCATION

Idaho State University College of Pharmacy Pocatello, Idaho	Doctor of Pharmacy degree August 2009–May 2013
University of Nevada at Reno Reno, Nevada	Pre-Pharmacy Curriculum September 2006–June 2009

EXPERIENCE

Boise VA Medical Center Boise, Idaho	Clinical Pharmacist August 2014–Present
Veterans Affairs Medical Center 8740 South Harbor Boulevard Harbor City, California	Primary Care Pharmacy Practice Residency July 2013–June 2014
St. Mary's Hospital Reno, Nevada	Pharmacy Intern Summers, 2010 and 2011
Walgreens Pharmacy Reno, Nevada	Pharmacy Technician July 2007–July 2009 Part-time
Nevada Seismological Laboratory University of Nevada at Reno Reno, Nevada	Transcription Technician October 2006–June 2007 Part-time

Actual CV size is 8.5 × 11 inches.

CV 1 Ryan David Freeman, Page 2 of 5

Ryan David Freeman
Curriculum Vitae, Page 2

PHARMACY PRACTICE EXPERIENCE ROTATIONS

Primary Care Pharmacy Residency
Veterans Affairs Medical Center, Harbor City, California

- Required Rotation – 9 months

  Ambulatory Care Clinic
  Preceptor: Michael Ko, Pharm.D.

- Elective Rotations – 2 months

  Santa Ana Family Medicine Center
  Santa Ana, California
  Preceptor: Jeannette Livingston, Pharm.D.

  Jackson Healthcare Nursing Home
  Fullerton, California
  Preceptor: Marian Baker, Pharm.D.

- Concurrent Rotations – 4 hours per week for 10 months

  Anticoagulation Clinic
  Preceptor: Michael Ko, Pharm.D.

  Infectious Diseases Clinic
  Preceptor: Krisin Barnes, Pharm.D.

Doctor of Pharmacy Degree Program
Idaho State University, Pocatello, Idaho

- Required Rotations – 7 months

  Hospital Pharmacy Practice
  Moreno Valley Community Hospital, Moreno Valley, California
  Preceptor: Lisa Moore, M.S., R.Ph.

  Internal Medicine
  Irvine Medical Center, Irvine, California
  Preceptor: Tracey Chan, Pharm.D.

Actual CV size is 8.5 × 11 inches.

CV 1 Ryan David Freeman, Page 3 of 5

Ryan David Freeman
Curriculum Vitae, Page 3

Doctor of Pharmacy Degree Program (Continued)
Idaho State University, Pocatello, Idaho

- Required Rotations – 7 months

  Community Pharmacy Practice
  Albertsons Pharmacy, Irvine, California
  Preceptor: Kamy Lee, Pharm.D.

  Primary Care
  Kaiser Permanente Hospital, San Diego, California
  Preceptor: Jason Neu, Pharm.D.

  Psychiatry
  Pocatello Regional Medical Center, Pocatello, Idaho
  Preceptor: Thao Nguyen, Pharm.D.

  Drug Information
  Pocatello Regional Medical Center, Pocatello, Idaho
  Preceptor: Harold Weiss, Pharm.D.

- Elective Rotations – 2 months

  Infectious Diseases
  Pocatello Regional Medical Center, Pocatello, Idaho
  Preceptor: Courtney Scott, Pharm.D.

  Administration
  Idaho Board of Pharmacy, Pocatello, Idaho
  Preceptor: Frederick Hamilton, R.Ph.

LICENSES

Idaho State Board of Pharmacy – 2013	Pharmacist No. 1138, examination
California State Board of Pharmacy – 2013	Pharmacist No. 013772, examination
Nevada Board of Pharmacy – 2014	Pharmacist No. 4961, reciprocity

Actual CV size is 8.5 × 11 inches.

CV 1 Ryan David Freeman, Page 4 of 5

Ryan David Freeman
Curriculum Vitae, Page 4

Publications

Freeman RD, Ko MA, Young HF. An analysis of pharmaceutical care outcome measures in patients receiving antiretroviral drug therapy. *Am J Health-Syst Pharm.* In Press.

Freeman RD. The pharmacists role in wellness and disease prevention. *Idaho Pharmacist.* 2011; 49:24–27.

Selected Presentations

June 2016	"The Pharmacists Role in Wellness and Disease Prevention" presented to members of the Idaho Pharmaceutical Association, Pocatello, Idaho.
October 2015	"Perspectives on Immunization Therapy" presented at Medical Grand Rounds, Boise VA Medical Center, Boise, Idaho.
December 2014	"The Evaluation of Pharmaceutical Care Outcome Measures in Patients Receiving Antiretroviral Drug Therapy" presented as a poster at the American Society of Health-System Pharmacists Midyear Clinical Meeting, Atlanta, Georgia.
October 2014	"Minimizing the Adverse Effects of Oral Anticoagulation Therapy" presented at Medical Grand Rounds, Veterans Affairs Medical Center, Harbor City, California.
May 2014	"An evaluation of the Pharmacoeconomic Impact of Pharmacist Interventions in an Infectious Diseases Clinic" presented at the Western Pharmacy Residency Conference, Anaheim, California.
April 2014	"Drug Management of Prostatitis" presented to Team II medical residents and interns at the Veterans Affairs Medical Center, Harbor City, California.
February 2014	"Novel Drug Therapies for the Management of HIV/AIDS Patients" presented to members of the Departments of Nursing and Pharmacy at the Veterans Affairs Medical Center, Harbor City, California.
December 2013	"Application of Knowledge in a Primary Care Pharmacy Practice Residency" presented to students and faculty at the University of Idaho College of Pharmacy, Pocatello, Idaho.

Actual CV size is 8.5 × 11 inches.

CV 1 Ryan David Freeman, Page 5 of 5

Ryan David Freeman
Curriculum Vitae, Page 5

Professional Memberships

American Society of Health-System Pharmacists	2013–Present
California Society of Health-System Pharmacists	2013–Present
Idaho Pharmacists Association	2009–Present
American Pharmacists Association	2009–Present

Leadership Experience

Idaho Pharmacists Association

- Treasurer 2015–2016
- Chairman, Membership Committee 2014–2015

Idaho State University School of Pharmacy

- Phi Delta Chi, President 2012–2013
- Phi Lambda Sigma, Treasurer 2011–2012
- Academy of Student Pharmacists, Vice President 2011–2012

Service Activities

American Cancer Society, Boise Idaho

- Coordinator, Great American Smoke-Out Event 2015

American Red Cross Blood Drive, Harbor City, California

- Team Captain, VA Medical Center March 2014

Boy Scouts of America, Reno, Nevada

- Leader, Troop 12 2010

Awards and Recognition

Veterans Affairs Medical Center, Harbor City, California

- Outstanding Resident Award 2014

Idaho State University, Pocatello, Idaho

- Outstanding Pharmacy Leader Award 2013
- J. Alan Simpson Scholarship 2012

References

Available upon request

Actual CV size is 8.5 × 11 inches.

CV 2 Ellen Lee Woodruff, Page 1 of 5

A CV for a community pharmacist in practice 12 years who also has hospital and teaching experience.
Font: Lucida Sans 12 point.

CURRICULUM VITAE

Ellen Lee Woodruff

942 Derbyshire Court
Tallahassee, Florida 32302
(850) 564-7820
elwood@advancelink.com
www.linkedin/in/elwoodruff

QUALIFICATIONS PROFILE

Pharmacist with eight years of community pharmacy practice and four years of hospital pharmacy practice
Taught high school chemistry for three years
Dedicated to community service activities

List of responsibilities is clear and concise; she could consider emphasizing and quantifying achievements in each position, such as "administer [number] immunizations per year" or "compound [number] medications annually."

PHARMACY PRACTICE EXPERIENCE

Jay's Apothecary 2013–Present
1210 South Point Boulevard
Tallahasee, Florida 32306
(850) 721-8000
Supervisor: Jay T. Roberts, Pharm.D.

Responsibilities: Participate in disease state management services for patients with asthma, diabetes and lipid disorders; administer immunizations; evaluate and dispense prescriptions for patients; counsel patients on the proper use of their medication and related devices; compound extemporaneous prescription products; and, precept pharmacy students and interns.

Coastal Pharmacy 2010–2012
859 Coastal Avenue
Oceanside, California 92052
(760) 345-9000
Supervisor: Bao H. Nguyen, Pharm.D.

Including supervisors' names is optional but not necessary, especially for someone with several years of practice experience. These could appear in a separate list of references.

Actual CV size is 8.5 × 11 inches.

CV 2 Ellen Lee Woodruff, Page 2 of 5

Ellen Lee Woodruff
Curriculum Vitae
Page 2

PHARMACY PRACTICE EXPERIENCE (Continued)

Responsibilities: Compounded prescriptions in specific dosage forms for human and veterinary use; demonstrated the proper use of compounding equipment and related devices; promoted the availability of compounding services to physicians and other healthcare professionals in the community; evaluated and dispensed prescriptions for patients; and, counseled patients on the proper use of their medication and related devices; and assisted in the precept of pharmacy interns.

Rite Aid Pharmacy 2009–2010
1800 Vista Way
Oceanside, California 92056
(760) 722-2040
Pharmacist in Charge: Elaine Magee, R.Ph.

Responsibilities: Received and interpreted written prescriptions from prescribers; determined health plan eligibility for patients; dispensed medication; maintained computer records of prescriptions dispensed; maintained a health information display center containing printed health information materials for the public; and, counseled patients on the proper use of their medication and related devices.

Walgreens Pharmacy 2008–2009
10875 Poway Highway
Poway, California 92074
(858) 745-6700
Pharmacist in Charge: Alice Chen, R.Ph.

Responsibilities: Received and interpreted written prescriptions from prescribers; determined health plan eligibility for patients; dispensed medication; maintained computer records of prescriptions dispensed; maintained an inventory of prescription and nonprescription drug products; and, counseled patients on the proper use of their medication and related devices.

Tacoma General Hospital 2004–2008
304 Madison Street
Tacoma, Washington 98356
(253) 812-3872
Pharmacist in Charge: Liang Yuen, Pharm.D.

Actual CV size is 8.5 × 11 inches.

CV 2 Ellen Lee Woodruff, Page 3 of 5

Ellen Lee Woodruff
Curriculum Vitae
Page 3

PHARMACY PRACTICE EXPERIENCE (Continued)

Responsibilities: Received and interpreted written prescriptions for hospitalized patients; reviewed prescription orders for potential drug interactions, allergies, or adverse events; reviewed prescription orders for formulary status and recommended therapeutic alternatives when appropriate; assured the accuracy of medication orders completed by pharmacy technicians; provided drug information services to physicians and nurses; prepared and dispensed small and large volume parenteral intravenous solutions; maintained an inventory of controlled substances and investigational drugs; provided medication counseling to patients at the time of their hospital discharge; and, assisted in the preparation of a monthly departmental newsletter.

PROFESSIONAL DEVELOPMENT

Professional Compounding Centers of America Continuing Education Program	2011 and 2014
Health Supports and Appliances Certification Program National Community Pharmacists Association	2013

EDUCATION

St. John's University, Jamaica, New York College of Pharmacy and Allied Health Programs Bachelor of Science in Pharmacy Degree Conferred	2000–2003
Onondaga Community College, Syracuse, New York Pre-Pharmacy Course Work Completed	1999–2000
Syracuse University School of Education and College of Arts and Sciences Syracuse, New York Bachelor of Science in Chemistry Degree Conferred	1988–1992

Actual CV size is 8.5 × 11 inches.

CV 2 Ellen Lee Woodruff, Page 4 of 5

Ellen Lee Woodruff
Curriculum Vitae
Page 4

LICENSES AND CERTIFICATES

Florida Board of Pharmacy (#12678, by examination)	2013
California State Board of Pharmacy (# 41689, by examination)	2008
Washington State Board of Pharmacy (# R-09737, by reciprocity)	2004
New York Board of Pharmacy (#19-027305, by examination)	2003
New York State Teaching Certificate	1992

TEACHING EXPERIENCE

Clinical Assistant Professor — 2015–Present
University of Florida, Gainesville, Florida

Clinical Assistant Professor — 2015–Present
Florida A and M University, Tallahassee, Florida

Practitioner-Teacher — 2011–2012
University of Southern California, Los Angeles,

Chemistry Teacher — 1992–1995
West Syracuse High School, Syracuse, New York

PRESENTATIONS

"Osteoporosis and You" presented to members of the Tallahassee Woman's Club, Tallahassee, Florida, October 2013

"Ostomy and Incontinence Care" presented to Oceanside Ostomy Support Group, Oceanside, California, April 2011

"Safety Rules for Your Medicine Cabinet" presented as an interview with WTCW-TV, Tacoma, Washington, February, 2006

"Smoking and Your Health" presented to members of the National Honor Society, Foxworth High School, Tacoma, Washington, October 2005

"Tips for Medication Childproofing Your Home" presented to members of the Powell Middle School Parent-Teachers Association, Tacoma, Washington, March 2005

Actual CV size is 8.5 × 11 inches.

CV 2 Ellen Lee Woodruff, Page 5 of 5

Ellen Lee Woodruff
Curriculum Vitae
Page 5

PROFESSIONAL AND COMMUNITY AFFILIATIONS

Florida Pharmacy Association	2013–Present
Tallahassee Woman's Club	2013–Present
National Community Pharmacists Association	2012–Present
Washington State Pharmacy Association • Member, Public Affairs Committee, 2001	2005–2008
American Institute of the History of Pharmacy	2005–Present
Powell Middle School Parent-Teacher's Association Tacoma, Washington • President, 2007–2008 • Vice-President, 2006–2007	2004–2008
Tacoma Woman's Club	2004–2008
American Pharmacists Association (formerly known as American Pharmaceutical Association)	2001–Present

AWARDS AND RECOGNITION

American Cancer Society Award for smoking cessation activities in the community, California	2004
Most Outstanding Member Award Tacoma Woman's Club	2008

REFERENCES

Provided Upon Request

Actual CV size is 8.5 × 11 inches.

CV 3 Mylinh Le Pham, Page 1 of 6

A concise, easy-to-read CV for a recent pharmacy graduate interested in academia.
Font: Times New Roman 11 and 12 point.

A summary statement at the beginning is optional but would be useful for highlighting this pharmacist's strengths, such as public speaking experience.

Mylinh Le Pham

Curriculum Vitae
May 2016

PERSONAL

Current Address	305 Parkland Road Richmond, Virginia 23235 804.781.8873 mlpham3@vcu.edu
Permanent Address	9149 Mill Court Drive Alexandria, Virginia 22314 703.549.2386 mylinh.pham@earthnet.com

CAREER GOAL

To pursue a non-tenure faculty position in pharmacy practice

EDUCATION

2011–2015	Virginia Commonwealth University Medical College of Virginia Campus School of Pharmacy Richmond, Virginia Doctor of Pharmacy degree Conferred: May 2015
2007–2011	Virginia Polytechnic Institute and State University, Blacksburg, Virginia B.S. in Biochemistry degree Conferred: May 2011

SPECIALIZED TRAINING

2015–2016	Community Pharmacy Practice Residency Virginia Commonwealth University School of Pharmacy Richmond, Virginia Program Director: John Harmon, Pharm.D. Certificate Awarded: May 2016

To highlight her unique skills, she could add a couple of bullet points with a bit more detail and some accomplishments in the sections on training, professional experience, research, and teaching.

Actual CV size is 8.5 × 11 inches.

CV 3 Mylinh Le Pham, Page 2 of 6

Mylinh Le Pham
Curriculum Vitae
Page 2

PROFESSIONAL EXPERIENCE

Pharmacy Practice Experiences (May 2014–May 2015)	Acute Care–Adult Medicine Medical College of Virginia Hospitals, Richmond, VA Preceptor: Barbara Muncy, Pharm.D.
	Primary Ambulatory Care Veteran's Administration Hospital, Richmond, VA Preceptor: William Morris, Pharm.D.
	Health-Systems Practice St. Mary's Hospital, Richmond, VA Preceptor: Francis Myles, Pharm.D.
	Community Practice Lynchburg Apothecary, Lynchburg, VA Preceptor: Lee Philips, R.Ph.
	Long-Term Care Ridgeview Nursing Center, Roanoke, VA Preceptor: Mary Tucker, R.Ph.
	Elective–Primary Ambulatory Care PHS Indian Health Center, Fort Duchesne, UT Preceptor: Howard Stewart, Pharm.D.
	Elective–Association Management Virginia Pharmacists Association, Richmond, VA Preceptor: Betty Schumaker, R.Ph.
	Elective–Psychiatry Medical College of Virginia Hospitals, Richmond, VA Preceptor: Tim Bolton, Pharm.D.
Internship (Summers 2012 & 2013)	Pharmacy Intern Tidwell Pharmacy, Alexandria, VA Preceptor: Julia Tidwell, R.Ph.
Employment (Summers 2010 & 2011)	Pharmacy Technician Alexandria Hospital, Alexandria, VA Preceptor: Hugh Chan

Actual CV size is 8.5 × 11 inches.

CV 3 Mylinh Le Pham, Page 3 of 6

Mylinh Le Pham
Curriculum Vitae
Page 3

LICENSES AND CERTIFICATES

July 2015–Present	Pharmacist, License No. 5862 Commonwealth of Virginia
April 2014–Present	Advanced Cardiac Life Support Provider American Heart Association

RESEARCH EXPERIENCE

September 2015–Present	Assessing the outcome of non-prescription medication use in a diabetic population

TEACHING EXPERIENCE

July 2015–Present	Instructor in Pharmacy Virginia Commonwealth University • Lecturer, PHAR-742 (Pharmacotherapy III) • Lecturer, PHAR-648 (Women's Health) • Preceptor, PHAR-766 (Community Ambulatory Care Practice)

PUBLICATIONS

2017	Pham ML, Toth HR. The consequences of non-prescription medication use in a diabetic population. *Am J Health-Syst Pharm.* Submitted for publication
2015	Pham ML. New strategies in managing allergic rhinitis. *Virginia Pharmacist* 2015; 88(7):24–26.

PRESENTATIONS

May 2016	"Managing non-prescription medication use for diabetic patients" presented to members of the Old Dominion Pharmaceutical Association, Lynchburg, Virginia.
April 2016	"Advances in devices to administer medications to asthmatics" presented to the nursing staff of the Visiting Nurses Association, Richmond, Virginia.

Actual CV size is 8.5 × 11 inches.

CV 3 Mylinh Le Pham, Page 4 of 6

Mylinh Le Pham
Curriculum Vitae
Page 4

PRESENTATIONS (Continued)

April 2016	"Dealing with drug formulary decision making" presented to physicians and staff of the Virginia Medical Associates, Fredericksburg, Virginia
February 2016	"The treatment of hyperlipidemia with lovastatin" presented to members of the Tidewater Pharmacists Association, Chesapeake, Virginia
January 2016	"Community Pharmacy Residency Programs" presented to members of the Class of 2011, VCU School of Pharmacy, Richmond, Virginia
November 2015	"The benefits of a pharmacy-based immunization program" presented to patients of the Buxton Place Pharmacy, Petersburg, Virginia
October 2015	"The use of low molecular weight heparin for ambulatory patients" presented to the pharmacy staff of St. John's Hospital, Johnson City, Virginia
August 2015	"Advances in treating asthma" presented to members of the Richmond Asthma Support Group, Richmond, Virginia
March 2015	"The treatment of gout and hyperuricemia" presented to students and faculty of the VCU School of Pharmacy, Richmond, Virginia

PROFESSIONAL MEMBERSHIPS

2014–Present	Rho Chi Pharmaceutical Honor Society
2013–2015	Student Chapter of the National Community Pharmacists Association
2013–2015	Student National Pharmaceutical Association
2012–Present	Kappa Epsilon Professional Pharmacy Fraternity
2011–Present	American Pharmacists Association
2011–Present	Virginia Pharmacists Association
2011–Present	American Society of Health-System Pharmacists
2011–2015	Virginia Academy of Student Pharmacists

Actual CV size is 8.5 × 11 inches.

CV 3 Mylinh Le Pham, Page 5 of 6

Mylinh Le Pham
Curriculum Vitae
Page 5

LEADERSHIP EXPERIENCE

2015–2016	Virginia Pharmacists Association • Member, Policy Committee
2014–2015	Kappa Epsilon Professional Pharmacy Fraternity • Vice-President
2013–2015	Virginia Academy of Student Pharmacists • President, 2014–2015 • Secretary, 2013–2014 • Alternate Delegate, 2013

COMMUNITY SERVICE

April 2016	Alzheimer's Association Memory Walk
March 2016	Richmond Pharmacists Association Health Fair
January 2016	Pharmacy Day 2010 at the Virginia Legislature
October 2015	Richmond Pharmacists Association Diabetes Screening Clinic
September 2015	WRVA Health Awareness Campaign
May 2015	American Cancer Society's Relay for Life
November 2014	Virginia Pharmacists Operation Immunization Project
September 2013	Poison Prevention Awareness Program at Chester Middle School, Chester, Virginia

AWARDS AND HONORS

2015	Pharmacy Communications Award
2015	American Pharmacists Association–Academy of Student Pharmacists Mortar and Pestle Award
2014	Johnson Academic Scholarship
2012–2015	Dean's List of Outstanding Students (Fall and Spring semesters)

Actual CV size is 8.5 × 11 inches.

CV 3 Mylinh Le Pham, Page 6 of 6

Mylinh Le Pham
Curriculum Vitae
Page 6

The list of references at the end is not customary, but you can add such a list if you choose.

REFERENCES

John Harmon, Pharm.D.
Professor of Pharmacy
School of Pharmacy
Virginia Commonwealth University
410 North 12th Street
Richmond, Virginia 23298-0674
Telephone: (804) 828-4976
E-mail: jaharmon@vcu.edu

Judith R. Townsend, Pharm.D.
Assistant Professor of Pharmacy
School of Pharmacy
Virginia Commonwealth University
410 North 12th Street
Richmond, Virginia 23298-0674
Telephone: (804) 828-3129
E-mail: jrtownse@vcu.edu

Monica A. West, R.Ph.
Buxton Place Pharmacy
308 Buxton Place
Petersburg, Virginia 23803
Telephone: (804) 786-4000
E-mail: monica.west@snapnet.com

Frank C. Walker, M.D.
Associate Professor of Medicine
School of Medicine
Virginia Commonwealth University
1101 East Marshall Street
Richmond, Virginia 23298-0972
Telephone: (804) 828-0388
E-mail: fcwalker@vcu.edu

Actual CV size is 8.5 × 11 inches.

CV 4 Samantha Christine Lewis, Page 1 of 5

A CV for a student about to graduate who is looking for a hospital pharmacy residency.
Font: Lucida Bright 10, 11, and 12 point.

CURRICULUM VITAE

SAMANTHA CHRISTINE LEWIS

Local Residence
4990 Warren Street
Cincinnati, Ohio 45214
Phone: (513) 651-6022
E-Mail: sclewis@zipnet.com

Permanent Residence
4804 Lamar Boulevard
Dayton, Ohio 45406
Phone: (937) 277-9758

Quantifying key achievements, perhaps in a summary statement at the beginning, would give readers a snapshot of her strengths.

CAREER OBJECTIVE

To seek a pharmacy practice residency in a health-system pharmacy

EDUCATION

September 2010–Present

University of Cincinnati
James L. Winkle College of Pharmacy
Cincinnati, Ohio
Doctor of Pharmacy
Degree anticipated May 2010

Format allows readers to skim quickly.

Provides succinct descriptions of duties in each internship.

PROFESSIONAL EXPERIENCE

May 2011–Present

Pharmacy Intern
Christ Hospital, Cincinnati, Ohio
Preceptor: Elaine Curtis, R.Ph.

Activities include dispensing inpatient unit dose medications, responding to drug information requests from nurses, preparing intravenous admixtures including parenteral nutrition solutions and chemotherapy

July 2008–June 2010

Pharmacy Technician
Good Samaritan Hospital, Cincinnati, Ohio
Supervisor: Harold Gibson, R.Ph.

Activities included filling inpatient medication orders, preparing intravenous admixtures, compounding, and inventory functions for controlled substances

April 2005–April 2008

Pharmacy Clerk
Kroger Pharmacy, Ft. Mitchell, Kentucky
Supervisor: Tricia Stevens

Activities included processing insurance claims, maintaining inventory and cashier duties

Actual CV size is 8.5 × 11 inches.

CV 4 Samantha Christine Lewis, Page 2 of 5

SAMANTHA CHRISTINE LEWIS PAGE 2

PHARMACY PRACTICE ROTATIONS

March 2016-April 2016

Elective - Acute Care - Infectious Diseases
University Hospital, Cincinnati, Ohio
Preceptor: Elizabeth Crowder, Pharm.D.

Activities included daily rounds with Infectious Disease Consult Service, monitoring and assessing the appropriateness of antibiotic therapy, conducting patient medication histories, performing pharmacokinetics calculations for dosage recommendations of antibiotics, patient counseling

February 2016-March 2016

Primary Ambulatory Care
Browning's Pharmacy, Montgomery, Ohio
Preceptor: Todd Edmonds, Pharm.D.

Activities included assisting with the development of a smoking cessation program, monitoring the drug therapy of patients with chronic diseases, responding to drug information requests from physicians and nurses, documenting patient interventions, processing and dispensing prescriptions

January 2016-February 2016

Nursing Home Practice
Schwartz Pharmacy, Cincinnati, Ohio
Preceptor: Suzanna Ward, R.Ph.

Activities included administering immunizations, stocking automated dispensing devices, conducting monthly nursing home chart reviews, reviewing medication pass procedures with nurses, attending quality assurance committee meetings

November 2015-December 2015

Community Practice
Walgreens Pharmacy, Covington, Kentucky
Preceptor: Terry Barker, R.Ph.

Activities included preparing and dispensing prescription medications, receiving verbal prescriptions from physicians, counseling patients about prescription medications, assessing and recommending non-prescription medications

Actual CV size is 8.5 × 11 inches.

CV 4 Samantha Christine Lewis, Page 3 of 5

PHARMACY PRACTICE ROTATIONS (Continued)

October 2015-November 2015

Elective - General Surgery
University Hospital, Cincinnati, Ohio
Preceptor: Julie Wright, Pharm.D.

Activities included attending daily rounds with a general surgery team, monitoring drug therapy, developing drug therapy treatment plans, participating in a drug usage evaluation of vancomycin therapy

September 2015-October 2015

Acute Care - Oncology
University Hospital, Cincinnati, Ohio
Preceptor: Rebecca Reaves, Pharm.D.

Activities included monitoring and assessing the appropriateness of chemotherapy, assisting with record keeping for investigational chemotherapeutic agents, assisting in the collection of data for a drug usage evaluation for ondansetron therapy, attending multidisciplinary team meetings for the discharge planning of patients

August 2015-September 2015

Acute Care - Medicine
St. Luke Hospital - East, Ft. Thomas, Kentucky
Preceptor: William Crowder, Pharm.D.

Activities included attending daily rounds with physicians, conducting patient medication histories, performing pharmacokinetics dosage calculations for selected drugs, responding to drug information requests from nurses and physicians, detecting and reporting adverse drug reactions,

July 2015-August 2015

Health-System Practice
Fort Hamilton Hospital, Hamilton, Ohio
Preceptor: Jason Friedman, R.Ph.

Activities included entering physician orders into computer system, filling inpatient medication orders, delivering unit dose cassettes to patient care areas, preparing intravenous admixture solutions, conducting an in-service education program for nurses, conducting nursing unit inspections, responding to drug information requests

Actual CV size is 8.5 × 11 inches.

CV 4 Samantha Christine Lewis, Page 4 of 5

PHARMACY PRACTICE ROTATIONS (Continued)

June 2015-July 2015

Acute Care - Medicine
University Hospital, Cincinnati, Ohio
Preceptor: Sarah Nichols, Pharm.D.

Activities included attending daily rounds with adult medicine team, monitoring drug therapy for assigned patients and making recommendations to preceptor and team, assisting in the collection of data for a drug usage evaluation

CERTIFICATES and LICENSES

2013-Present

Basic Life Support Provider
American Heart Association

2011-Present

Pharmacy Intern License No. 4698
Ohio Board of Pharmacy

PROFESSIONAL MEMBERSHIPS

2010-Present

University of Cincinnati
Academy of Student Pharmacists

2010-Present

American Pharmacists Association

2010-Present

Ohio Pharmacists Association

2011-Present

Kappa Epsilon

- President, 2014–2015
- Secretary, 2013–2014
- Chaplain, 2012–2013

PRESENTATIONS

April 2016

"Reducing Occupational Exposure to Bloodborne Pathogens" presented to faculty and students, College of Pharmacy

October 2015

"Cyclosporine therapy" presented to faculty and students, College of Pharmacy

July 2015

"Drug Management of Pregnancy-Induced Hypertension" presented to medical team and 3 West nursing staff, University Hospital

Actual CV size is 8.5 × 11 inches.

CV 4 Samantha Christine Lewis, Page 5 of 5

SAMANTHA CHRISTINE LEWIS PAGE 5

COMMUNITY SERVICE

2016	Kappa Epsilon Easter Egg Hunt Simpson Elementary School, Hamilton, Ohio
2015	Project Angel Tree Salvation Army, Newport, Kentucky
2013-2014	Volunteer, Habitat for Humanity
Summer 2012	Counselor, Camp Juniper for Girls Madison, Ohio

AWARDS AND HONORS

2015	Finalist, Patient Counseling Competition U.C. Academy of Student Pharmacists
2015-Present	Member, Phi Lambda Sigma
2010	Elks Foundation Scholarship

REFERENCES

Available upon request

Actual CV size is 8.5 × 11 inches.

CV 5 Marianna Alicia Garcia, Page 1 of 4

A readable, nicely designed CV for a pharmacist currently involved in a pharmacy practice fellowship.
Font: Century Schoolbook 10 and 12 point.

CURRICULUM VITAE

Marianna Alicia Garcia

Local Address	**Permanent Address**
3663 Madison Place	7320 Lakewood Drive
Chicago, Illinois 60619	Springfield, Illinois 62702
(773) 846-6092	(217) 522-5164
E-mail: garcia08@uic.edu	

Education

University of Illinois at Chicago College of Pharmacy Chicago, Illinois	Doctor of Pharmacy Degree awarded June 2013
University of Illinois at Springfield Springfield, Illinois	Pre-Pharmacy Curriculum September 2006–June 2009

Specialized Training

Industrial Pharmacy Practice Fellowship	Hoffmann-La Roche, Inc. Nutley, New Jersey and Rutgers University Ernest Mario School of Pharmacy Piscataway, New Jersey Certificate expected June 2017
Specialized Residency in Drug Information Practice	University of Illinois at Chicago College of Pharmacy Chicago, Illinois Certificate awarded June 2015
Pharmacy Practice Residency	St. John's Hospital Chicago, Illinois Certificate awarded June 2014

Actual CV size is 8.5 × 11 inches.

CV 5 Marianna Alicia Garcia, Page 2 of 4

Marianna Alicia Garcia Page 2

Professional Experience

Industrial Pharmacy Practice Fellowship
2015–2017

Hoffman-La Roche, Inc., Clinical Pharmacology Department and Rutgers University

Experience Gained:

- Participated in protocol design
- Developed case report forms
- Selected investigators and sites
- Prepared operating budgets
- Participated in contract negotiations
- Monitored study sites
- Reviewed drug supply management procedures
- Managed data and conducted analyses
- Plan to prepare final study reports
- Plan to develop professional product information
- Plan to participate in research quality assurance

Here, the "Experience Gained" sections make proper use of action verbs in a concise listing.

Specialized Residency in Drug Information Practice
2014–2015

University of Illinois at Chicago College of Pharmacy

Experience Gained:

- Developed a plan to establish a drug information service
- Designed a plan for documenting the impact of a drug information service
- Developed selected medication use policies and procedures
- Participated in drug information service quality assurance
- Prepared drug literature evaluations in support of formulary management, disease state management guidelines and drug therapy guidelines
- Prepared and edited newsletters for health professionals
- Participated in medication error and adverse drug reaction monitoring and reporting activities
- Conducted medication use evaluations
- Performed financial and clinical outcomes analyses

Actual CV size is 8.5 × 11 inches.

CV 5 Marianna Alicia Garcia, Page 3 of 4

Professional Experience (Continued)

Pharmacy Practice Residency
2013–2014

St. John's Hospital
Chicago, Illinois

Practice Experience Gained:

- Adult internal medicine
- Pain service
- Drug information
- Hematology/oncology
- Infectious diseases
- Pediatrics
- Home infusion service
- Pharmacy administration
- Ambulatory patient care

Listings of rotations are fine, but some employers appreciate a bit more detail about what was unique or exceptional about the experience.

Doctor of Pharmacy Program
2009–2013

University of Illinois at Chicago
College of Pharmacy

Practice Experience Gained:

- General medicine
- Psychiatry
- Administration
- Community Practice
- Ambulatory Care
- Hospital Practice
- Drug Information

Licensure and Certification

Board of Pharmacy Specialties — Pharmacotherapy Specialist, 2015–Present

New Jersey Board of Pharmacy — Pharmacist, License No. 2187, 2009

Illinois Board of Pharmacy — Pharmacist, License No. 3378, 2008

Academic Appointments

Rutgers University
Ernest Mario School of Pharmacy

Clinical Assistant Professor
2015–Present

University of Illinois at Chicago
College of Pharmacy

Instructor in Pharmacy
2013–2015

Actual CV size is 8.5 × 11 inches.

CV 5 Marianna Alicia Garcia, Page 4 of 4

Marianna Alicia Garcia Page 4

Publications

Garcia MA, Williamson TN. Resolving Medicare reimbursement issues for the use of prodrugs. *Pharmacotherapy*. 2016; 25:251–257.

Garcia MA, Johnson CR, Freeman PK. Cost-effectiveness of capecitabine versus anthracycline-containing chemotherapy regimens in the treatment of metastatic breast cancer. *Pharmacotherapy*. 2015; 24:957–962.

Garcia MA, Sniderman HJ. The impact of pharmacoeconomic research on reimbursement policies. *Med Care*. 2015; 42:514–520.

Presentations at National Meetings

Garcia MA. *Reimbursement strategies for the use of prodrugs*. Paper presented at Washington: Annual Meeting of the American Pharmacists Association; March 2016.

Garcia MA. *Drug therapy options for patients with metastatic breast cancer*. Poster presented at Kansas City: Annual Meeting of the American College of Clinical Pharmacy; July 2015.

Current Professional Affiliations

American College of Clinical Pharmacy
American Pharmacists Association
(formerly American Pharmaceutical Association)
Drug Information Association
American Society of Health-System Pharmacists

Awards and Recognition

Chief Pharmacy Resident, University of Illinois at Chicago College of Pharmacy, 2014–2015
Phi Kappa Phi, University of Illinois, 2013
Patient Care Award, University of Illinois at Chicago College of Pharmacy, 2013
Leon J. Schwartz Scholarship, University of Illinois at Chicago College of Pharmacy, 2012
Rho Chi Honor Society, Phi Chapter, University of Illinois, 2011

Actual CV size is 8.5 × 11 inches.

CV 6 Glenn Michael Richards, Page 1 of 4

Condensed version of an academic CV for a tenured professor shows a useful way of listing grants, publications, and presentations. Font: Verdana 11 and 10 point.

Because CVs are updated many times over the course of a career, including the year affirms for readers that this is the most current version.

Curriculum Vitae
2016

Note: This is a condensed version of a 47-page curriculum vitae

Glenn Michael Richards

PERSONAL INFORMATION

Home Address:	4350 Old Lexington Road Athens, Georgia 30608 Telephone: 706-469-6683 E-mail: glenn.richards@earthlink.com Website: tinyurl.com/grichards
Office Address:	College of Pharmacy The University of Georgia Athens, Georgia 30602 Telephone: (706) 542-5278 Telefax: (706) 542-7652 E-mail: gmrichar@rx.uga.edu
Birthplace:	New Haven, Massachusetts
Nationality:	United States Citizen

EDUCATION

1985–1989	Doctor of Philosophy, Medicinal Chemistry State University of New York, School of Pharmacy, Buffalo, New York
1983–1985	Master of Science, Medicinal Chemistry Northeastern University College of Pharmacy, Boston, Massachusetts
1978–1983	Bachelor of Science, Pharmacy Northeastern University College of Pharmacy, Boston, Massachusetts

POSTDOCTORAL EXPERIENCE

1989–1991	Alcohol, Drug Abuse, Mental Health Administration Postdoctoral Fellow in Psychopharmacology, Department of Pharmacology and Experimental Therapeutics, State University of New York School of Medicine, Buffalo, New York

Actual CV size is 8.5 × 11 inches.

CV 6 Glenn Michael Richards, Page 2 of 4

Glenn Michael Richards
Curriculum vitae
Page 2

PROFESSIONAL POSITIONS

Department of Medicinal Chemistry, College of Pharmacy, The University of Georgia

- 2014–Present Chair
- 1999–Present Professor with Tenure
- 1996–1999 Associate Professor with Tenure
- 1991–1996 Assistant Professor

Department of Pharmacology and Toxicology, School of Medicine, The University of Georgia

- 2002–Present Affiliate Professor

Bon Secours Hospital, Boston, Massachusetts

- 1984–1985 Staff Pharmacist (Part-time)

Warner-Lambert Research Institute, Morris Plains, New Jersey

- 1983–1984 Research Chemist

HONORS

American Association of Colleges of Pharmacy

- Volwiler Research Achievement Award, 2015

American Pharmacists Association

- Research Achievement Award, 2012

The University of Georgia

- Distinguished Scholar Award, 2009

The University of Georgia School of Pharmacy

- Professor of the Year Award, 1995 and 2000

RESEARCH EXPERIENCE (2016)

Grants (approved and funded)

- Chemical/behavioral studies on hallucinogenic agents, National Institutes of Health, $459,840.
- Development of novel serotonin agonists, Alza Laboratories, $112,755.
- Designing mechanism-based agonists for selected hallucinogens, National Science Foundation, $88,227.

Patents

- Richards GM, Snider TA, Johnson FB. Signal serotonin modifier compounds, U.S. Patent No. 7,258,559 (June 15, 2016).

Actual CV size is 8.5 × 11 inches.

CV 6 Glenn Michael Richards, Page 3 of 4

Glenn Michael Richards
Curriculum vitae
Page 3

RESEARCH EXPERIENCE (2010) – Continued

Theses Supervised (Major Advisor)

- 18. Harold J. Niemeyer. Discriminative stimulus properties of hallucinogens and related designer drugs, Ph.D. in Pharmaceutical Sciences degree awarded May 2016.

PUBLICATIONS (2016)

Articles in Peer-reviewed Journals

- 274. Richards GM, Long RA, Johnson TE, Bunker PY. 2-Substituted tryptamines: Agents with selectivity for 5-HT6 receptors. *J. Med. Chem.* 48:1042–1049, 2016.
- 273. Young SC, Richards GM, Fong AN, Khun PK, Davis HW, Bond CK, Gerber HD. (+) Amphetamine stimulus generalization to an herbal ephedrine product. *Pharmacol. Biochem. Behav*. 70: 445–448, 2016.
- 272. Martin WR, Constantine DV, Jacobs IL, Sessler JL. Richards GM. A highly conserved aspartic acid (Asp-155) anchors the terminal amine moiety of tryptamines and is involved in membrane targeting of the 5-HT serotonin receptor. *J. Pharmacol. Exp. Ther*. 298: 884–889, 2016.
- 271. Heltzer NT, Richards GM, Ringley OC, Krueger TT. Central nicotinic receptor ligands and pharmacophores. *Pharm. Acta Helv*. 84:66–79, 2016.
- 270. Richards GM, Johnson TE, Jacobs IL. Binding of b-carbolines and related agents at serotonin (5-HT_2 and 5-HT_{3C}), dopamine and benzodiazepine receptors. *Psychopharmacology*. 155:305–316 (2016).
- 269. Sliaken VA, Washington PK, Richards GM, Darson KM. 1-[4-(2-Phenylalkyl)phenyl]-2-aminopropanes as 5-HT_{3C} partial agonists. *J. Med. Chem*. 70: 786–794, 2016.
- 268. Wong XJ, Bond MI, Malhumariart RB, Richards GM. Binding of spiperone analogs at 5-HT_{2A} serotonin receptors. *Eur. J. Pharmacol*. 389: 34–41, 2016.
- 267. Johnson TE, Fong AN, Richards GM, Gerber SN. Serotonin receptor binding or indolealkylamines: A preliminary structure-affinity investigation. *Med. Chem. Res.* 15: 128–134, 2016.

Invited Book Chapters

- 43. Richards GM. Neurobiology of hallucinogens, in *Handbook of Substance Abuse: Neurobehavioral Pharmacology*. Basel: Springer Verlag, 2016.

INVITED PRESENTATIONS (2016)

- 89. Serotonin receptor subtypes, 25th Annual International Symposium on Substance Abuse, Tokyo, Japan, May 2016.
- 88. Serotonin receptors and drugs affecting neurotransmission, University of Zurich, Zurich, Switzerland, March 2016.

Actual CV size is 8.5 × 11 inches.

CV 6 Glenn Michael Richards, Page 4 of 4

Glenn Michael Richards
Curriculum vitae
Page 4

TEACHING EXPERIENCE (2016)

- MEDC-526, Research Techniques in Medicinal Chemistry, lecturer, Spring 2016.
- MEDC-603, Medicinal Chemistry II, course coordinator, Spring 2016.
- MEDC-604, Medicinal Chemistry III, lecturer, Fall 2016.

SERVICE ACTIVITIES (2016)

National

- Member, National Advisory Council on Drug Abuse, Department of Health and Human Services, National Institutes of Health, National Institute on Drug Abuse
- Chair-elect, Medicinal and Natural Products Chemistry Section, American Association of Pharmaceutical Scientists
- Member, Awards Committee, American Association of Pharmaceutical Scientists

State

- Member, Georgia Council on Substance Abuse

University

- Member, Executive Budget Committee
- Vice-Chair, Health Sciences Research Space Advisory Committee
- Member, Search Committee for Chair of the Department of Chemistry

College

- Member, Strategic Planning Committee
- Member, Space Planning Committee
- Member, Academic Performance Committee
- Member, Scholarship and Awards Committee

PROFESSIONAL MEMBERSHIPS (2016)

- American Association of Colleges of Pharmacy
- American Pharmacists Association
- American Association of Pharmaceutical Scientists
- American Chemical Society
- American Association for the Advancement of Science
- Rho Chi Honor Society
- Phi Kappa Phi Honor Society

REFERENCES

Available upon request

Actual CV size is 8.5 × 11 inches.

CHAPTER 8

Developing a Portfolio for Electronic and Social Media

Artists and teachers have used portfolios for years to organize and document their professional growth. Pharmacy professionals can use this medium to highlight their progressive knowledge and skills. In fact, a portfolio gives a "show and tell" perspective of your experience and accomplishments. Just as you add information to your résumé and curriculum vitae, make a habit of adding samples of your work and examples of your achievements to your portfolio as you progress in your career. Items for inclusion might be details about your experiential training, internships, project samples, research findings, credentials, and photographs.

A portfolio gives a "show and tell" perspective of your experience and accomplishments.

Portfolio Design

How you design your portfolio will depend on the intended audience. Always include examples of your work that highlight the knowledge and skills relevant to the position you seek. Also, include an outline or index of the information in your portfolio. This feature will convey a neat, concise, and professional image.

Keep in mind that it is a portfolio, not a scrapbook, so avoid making it "cute" and stick to business-like graphics, headers, colors, and text fonts. A portfolio is not the place for hot pink paper or photographs mounted on doilies. Office supply stores sell binders and portfolio cases in which you can insert transparent, three-hole-punched sheet protectors to display your materials.

Because of the large amount of information contained in a typical portfolio, you may want to consider preparing an electronic version that can be shared in a flash drive format or through the internet. Preparation of an electronic portfolio (ePortfolio) and social media applications will be discussed later in this chapter.

Representative Components of a Portfolio

Personal Information

Begin your portfolio with your résumé or curriculum vitae. Consider including a personal statement that reflects your goals and objectives. If desired, this statement can summarize your commitment to a professional practice philosophy, teaching philosophy, or research and scholarship philosophy.

To enhance the personal nature of your portfolio, you may want to include a photograph and provide a list of your mentors and the assistance they provided in your professional development. Including a list of your personal interests reflects your ability to balance work and leisure time.

Education

You may find it helpful to include a separate section in your portfolio for your education. List the universities and colleges that you attended along with the degree or degrees you earned. If you completed a graduate degree, describe your graduate thesis and provide a brief biographical sketch of your major professor. You can also include transcripts from your college work as well as a photograph of your diploma and possibly other academic-related certificates.

Experiential Learning

One degree requirement for pharmacists is acquiring experiential learning, which can range from internships to postgraduate training experiences. Depending on your stage of professional development, you may want to amplify the areas of your most current training.

For example, a pharmacy student could list internships and advanced practice experience (i.e., clerkships) along

Educational Outcomes a Portfolio Can Highlight

1. *Patient-Centered Care*. Provide patient-centered care as the medication expert (collect and interpret evidence, prioritize, formulate assessments and recommendations, implement, monitor and adjust plans, document activities).
   - Collect subjective and objective evidence related to patient, medications, allergies/adverse reactions, and disease by performing patient assessment (including physical assessment) from chart/electronic health records, pharmacist records, and patient/family interviews.
   - Interpret evidence and patient data.
   - Prioritize patient needs.
   - Formulate evidence-based care plans, assessments, and recommendations.
   - Implement patient care plans.
   - Monitor the patient and adjust care plan as needed with supporting documentation.
2. *Medication Use Systems Management*. Manage patient health care needs using human, financial, technological, and physical resources to optimize the safety and efficacy of medication use systems.
   - Describe the pharmacist's role in impacting the safety and efficacy of each component of a typical medication use system (i.e., procurement, storage, prescribing, transcription, dispensing, administration, monitoring, documentation).
   - Utilize technology to optimize the medication use system.
   - Identify and utilize human, financial, and physical resources to optimize the medication use system.
   - Manage health care needs of patients during transitions of care.
   - Apply standards, guidelines, best practices, and established processes related to safe and effective medication use.
   - Utilize continuous quality improvement techniques in the medication use process.
3. *Health and Wellness*. Design preventive, interventional, and educational strategies for individuals and communities to manage chronic disease and to improve health and wellness.
   - Describe systematic preventive care using risk assessment, risk reduction, screening, education, and immunizations.
   - Provide preventive, interventional, and educational strategies for individuals and communities to improve health and wellness.
   - Participate with interprofessional health care team members in the management of, and health promotion for, all patients.
   - Evaluate personal, social, economic, and environmental conditions to maximize health and wellness.
4. *Population-Based Care*. Describe how population-based care influences patient-centered care and influences the development of practice guidelines and evidence-based best practices.
   - Assess the health care status and needs of a targeted patient population.
   - Develop and provide an evidence-based approach that considers the cost, care, access, and satisfaction needs of a targeted patient population.
   - Participate in population health management by evaluating and adjusting interventions to maximize health.

Source: Adapted from the *American Association of Colleges of Pharmacy Center for the Advancement of Pharmacy Education. Educational Outcomes, 2013.* Alexandria, VA: American Association of Colleges of Pharmacy; 2013.

with the name of the practice site, preceptor, description of duties and responsibilities, and preceptor evaluations. Use discretion in including evaluations, however, because you want to ensure that favorable impressions of your performance are provided.

A pharmacy resident may choose to describe residency rotations and to eliminate extensive information about advanced practice experiences gained as a pharmacy student. After practicing for several years, you can simply list the latter experiences in your curriculum vitae. After several years of practice, you might also choose to eliminate your introductory and advanced pharmacy practice rotations.

Recognition

Describing any kind of recognition you have received adds value to your portfolio. If you have received an award, for example, provide its title and a few words about its purpose, such as "for community service." You can enhance this listing by including a photograph of you receiving the recognition, a news clip about the award, or a visual image of the actual award.

Licensure/Certification

Pharmacy technicians, students, and practicing pharmacists all must have specific certifications or licenses for employment in a pharmacy. In this section of the portfolio, you can describe such certifications and even include a photograph of the documents. Or you can include a letter from the accrediting agency that documented your completion of a specific course or examination.

Professional Development Position Summaries

Highlight your professional development by including information about positions you have held. Provide summary statements about specific positions or include copies of the position description. In addition, consider adding a summary of your performance evaluations or a copy of these documents.

Service, Teaching, and Research

The service, teaching, and research triad can serve as a template for organizing your activities related to professional development. Focus areas can range from patient care to professional leadership.

If you are involved in teaching, include relevant samples. A preceptor can describe his or her advanced practice experience and provide copies of student evaluations. For faculty members, this section can include course syllabi, peer reviewer comments about your teaching, lecture outlines, videotaped presentations, and samples of student assignments.

Research or scholarly activities will vary with your background. For some people, such as faculty members, this section may include information about grants, publications, and invited presentations. For others, the section might include an article prepared for a newsletter or the outline of a technician training program prepared for a community college course.

National Pharmacy Standards

Still another approach involves organizing your professional development section around specific standards published by national pharmacy organizations. For example, a pharmacy resident can match his or her knowledge and skills against published standards for the specific type of residency program and then indicate how he or she met each competency. Similarly, a pharmacy student can correlate knowledge and skills with the educational outcomes developed by either the American Association of Colleges of Pharmacy's Center for the Advancement of Pharmacy Education or the professional competencies and outcome expectations required by the Accreditation Council for Pharmacy Education. The sidebar "Educational Outcomes a Portfolio Can Highlight" outlines some of these outcomes.

Memberships and Activities

The professional development section can also include a listing or description of your professional memberships, professional activities, areas of professional interest, consulting activities, and continuing education efforts.

Skills

Leadership

Most employers and program directors like to see evidence of leadership ability. You can demonstrate leadership potential by describing any elected or appointed positions you have held. Also, participation on a committee or team charged with completing a specific objective can show leadership abilities.

Communication

Effective communication skills are critical in every facet of the profession. Make sure you document evidence of your writing, speaking, and interpersonal communication successes. Include examples of oral presentations, written works, and situations in which you demonstrated strong interpersonal skills.

Information Technology

Systems for storing and sharing information continue to advance rapidly in the health care profession. To show potential employers that you stay current with these changes, consider

Portfolio Components

1. Personal Information
   - Name, designation, and title
   - Contact information
   - Mentors
   - Résumé or curriculum vitae
   - Personal statement
   - Photograph
   - Personal interests
2. Education
   - College or university attended
   - Degree(s) awarded
   - Major(s)
   - Graduate thesis and major professor
   - Academic record or transcript(s)
3. Licensure/Certification
   - Pharmacy licensure information
   - Specialty practice certification
   - Certificates of completion
4. Experiential Learning
   - Internship
   - Advanced practice experiences
   - Residency
   - Fellowship
   - Fulfillment of standards created by national organizations
5. Recognition
   - Scholarships
   - Academic honors
   - Awards
   - Certificates recognizing achievement
   - Letters recognizing achievement
6. Professional Development
   - Positions held and descriptions of duties
   - Performance evaluations
   - Service
     - Patient care
     - Community
     - School
     - University
     - Professional
   - Teaching
     - Lecture titles
     - Courses developed with syllabi
     - Courses coordinated with syllabi
     - Student evaluations
     - Peer reviewer comments
     - Sample of lecture outlines/slide presentations
     - Videotape of lecture(s) or segment(s)
     - Self-evaluation and description of improvement
     - Instructional strategies
     - Samples of students' work (e.g., exams, papers, projects)
   - Research/Scholarship
     - Areas of interest/expertise
     - Grants
     - Contracts
     - Projects
   - Publications
     - Abstracts
     - Articles
   - Presentations
     - Letters of invitation
     - Presentation evaluations
     - Sample handouts, slides, videos
     - Posters
   - Professional memberships
   - Professional activities
   - Professional interests
   - Consulting
   - Continuing education
7. Skills
   - Leadership
     - Elected positions
     - Appointed positions
     - Committee participation
     - Committee agendas
     - Documentation of outcomes
     - Team involvement
   - Communication
     - Oral presentations
     - Written works
     - Interpersonal skills
   - Computer
     - Software proficiency
     - Application of technology in teaching, research, and service
   - Professional practice
     - Patient case discussions
     - Evidence of problem solving
   - Management
     - Budget preparation
     - Human resource management
8. References
   - List of references and the significance of their relationship
   - Letters from colleagues

documenting your information technology skills. Describe your software proficiencies and explain how you apply technology in your teaching, research, and service activities.

Patient Care

Practicing pharmacists should consider highlighting their patient care skills. For example, document specific patient cases for which your problem-solving skills and professional intervention resulted in a positive outcome.

Management

Documenting evidence of budgetary involvement and human resource experience can help highlight management experience, especially if you seek work in this setting.

References

Include a list of references in your portfolio. Rather than merely listing names and contact information, you may want to describe the significance of each listed reference. For example, explain your relationship with each person and the type of insight that he or she can provide about your professional skills. Also, consider requesting general letters of reference from colleagues and mentors to include in your portfolio.

Preparing Your Portfolio for Electronic and Social Media Applications

The variety of digital tools available today makes the process of converting your paper portfolio to an electronic format an easy task. A starting point is to assemble materials to be included that are suitable for conversion to a digital format. In addition to print media, such as your career plan and curriculum vitae, you can consider photographs of your diplomas and certificates, slide sets for selected presentations, photographs associated with awards or recognitions, photographs of your participation in community service projects, publications, and audio-visual files of your presentations.

The next step is to select a website to create your ePortfolio. Many sites will host your ePortfolio free, although most such websites will have a sliding scale of charges based on the type and number of enhanced features. A listing of selected sites is included in Table 8.1. After creating an account, you will be prompted to create a title. Your first and last names are preferred to create a professional image. You also will be instructed to create a website domain that will serve as the link to your ePortfolio. Some sites will provide a domain free of charge by allowing you to use a subdomain. A better option that will enhance your professional image is to pay for a name with a domain registrar (e.g., https://www.gandi.net, http://www.namecheap.com) or with your web hosting site. Your host site will then provide instructions for designing the theme of your site and adding your content. Upon completion of these tasks, you can publish your portfolio and then add the website to your résumé, curriculum vitae, and other communications. It is important to routinely update your ePortfolio to maintain current information.

The information you assembled for your ePortfolio can be repurposed for other electronic social media sites, such

TABLE 8.1 Building Your ePortfolio

Website Host	Web Address	Comments/Features	Cost
Adobe Portfolio	https://www.myportfolio.com	Easy to use; templates	Tiered pricing
Google Sites	http://www.sites.google.com	Easy to use; long URL for free accounts; templates	Free
Squarespace	https://www.squarespace.com	Drag and drop feature; tutorials; dedicated support team; blog	Tiered pricing
Wix	https://www.wix.com	Drag and drop feature; templates	Free; tiered pricing for upgrades
Weebly	https://www.weebly.com	Drag and drop feature; templates	Free; tiered pricing for upgrades
WordPress	https://www.wordpress.com	Easy to use; easy to customize; built-in blog; templates; tutorials	Free; charge for domain name and hosting service
Yola	https://www.yola.com	Easy to use; templates; no third-party ads	Free; tiered pricing for upgrades

Key: URL = Uniform resource locator.

as LinkedIn. This site is characterized as a business network website, and many users tend to be affiliated with corporations; however, its number of profiles of pharmacists, pharmacy organizations and schools, and colleges of pharmacy is increasing. Registration is straightforward, requiring your e-mail address and creating a password. Directions are provided for creating a profile, which can include routine elements of your curriculum vitae (e.g., experience, education, skills, organizations), as well as the addition of your photograph. At a minimum, this website supports an organized file of contacts, effective networking among your contacts, and the opportunity to seek professional endorsements from your contacts.

Users can limit the types of notifications received and the degree of information shared with other users.

Some other social media sites may be considered for electronic networking. Facebook is the most popular networking site, because individuals, organizations, and universities frequently use the site to easily maintain professional connections. YouTube is useful for sharing videos with colleagues and can be linked to your ePortfolio. Other social media sites, including Twitter, Google+, Pinterest, Reddit, AboutMe, and SlideShare, are used routinely by pharmacy technicians, student pharmacists, and pharmacists. Professional ePortfolios can be linked to any of these websites to enhance one's personal brand.

CHAPTER 9

Preparing Letters

When you send out a résumé or curriculum vitae (CV), you also need to send a cover letter. A cover letter introduces you to the recipient and helps create an initial positive impression. As a marketing tool, the cover letter should highlight your qualifications, experience, and achievements, and it should also convince others that you deserve consideration for a position.

Although it is recommended to mail a cover letter with your résumé or CV, the letter and attachments can be sent electronically. The contents of the cover letter can be included as the body of the electronic message, or the letter can be included as an attachment along with the résumé or CV. If the latter method is chosen, the electronic message should be brief and appealing so the receiver will be prompted to open the attachments.

If possible, determine the name of the individual to receive your letter, and use the appropriate salutation to personalize the letter. If an individual is not identified, then the salutation can be "To Whom It May Concern."

The key question to which any employer ultimately wants an answer is "What can you do for us?" Cover letters are a great opportunity to highlight your special skills and experience and to suggest how they are relevant to the position you are applying for.

Tip: Letters are more effective when addressed to a specific person. If necessary, call the organization to obtain the name of the appropriate contact and the correct spelling of the name.

When well written, your cover letter helps distinguish you from other potential candidates. Keep your cover letters concise, clear, and to the point. Think of them as a supplement to your résumé or CV that answers important questions in the reader's mind, such as

- Why is this person writing?
- How well does his or her background meet the organization's needs?
- Does he or she have the qualifications needed for this position?

The Different Types of Job Search Letters

During your employment search process, you may need to send out various types of letters. As a general rule, you should type your letters. Thank you notes are the one exception, because handwritten notes seem more personal and genuine. However, you can type thank you letters when a more formal style seems appropriate.

Position Availability Inquiries

To research an organization that interests you and to learn of available positions, consider sending a letter of inquiry. Begin by explaining the reason for your letter, and state that your research or familiarity with the organization's reputation has prompted you to write. Summarize how your major achievements could benefit the organization. Express your thanks for being considered for positions that become available and conclude the letter by noting your availability for an interview. Attach your résumé or CV to round out the package.

Responding to a Position Notice

To express your interest in a position that was announced in an advertisement or job notice, start by explaining your reason for writing and how you learned about the available

Aspects of Great Cover Letters

To prepare the most effective cover letter:

- Address the letter to someone who has the authority to hire you. Use the person's name and title, spelled correctly.
- Keep the letter as brief and focused as possible.
- Tell how you became aware of the company or opportunity. Show that you have done some homework on the company by indicating that you understand their current problems, interests, or priorities.
- Convey your enthusiasm for the opportunity you seek.
- Balance a professional tone with touches of personal warmth. You do not want to sound like a machine.
- Outline specifically what responsibilities and challenges you are looking for and what skills and competencies you can offer.

position. Highlight your strengths and point out how they meet the requirements listed for the position. You will probably want to review your résumé or CV to choose those qualities that most closely match the stated requirements, but do not repeat wording verbatim. Instead, include your résumé or CV in the package. Before closing the letter, note your availability for an interview.

Requesting a Reference

Sometimes you will need a letter of recommendation from your references—people who can vouch for your skills and background and have agreed to be contacted. Although some potential employers prefer to make direct contact with references, others will ask you to supply written letters. Obtain these letters as soon as possible. Write a cover letter that expresses your appreciation for the person's willingness to serve as a reference and include the following information:

- Your résumé or CV
- A copy of the position announcement or description of duties
- A statement highlighting your additional, relevant qualifications for the position
- Specific contact information
- A deadline for completing the reference

Sometimes references will need to send their letters of recommendation directly to the potential employer. Other times you may need to submit the letters along with an application. In the second circumstance, ask each person preparing a reference to seal the letter in an envelope and sign his or her name across the sealed flap. Provide the reference with an addressed, stamped envelope for returning the recommendation to you or the potential employer.

Confirming an Interview

Sending a potential employer or program director an electronic message or a letter confirming your interview appointment reinforces the positive impression you have already made through your résumé, letters, and phone calls. It also demonstrates your attention to detail. Keep the letter very brief. Begin by expressing your appreciation for the opportunity to interview for the position. Then simply confirm the date, time, and location.

Thanking the Interviewer

After an interview, send a follow-up letter expressing your thanks, preferably within three days. Although a formal letter is preferred, an electronic message can be considered if you have previously communicated with the employer or program director via e-mail. Your letter should indicate your continuing interest in the position and highlight any specific areas that you consider relevant to discussions during the interview process. You may choose to comment briefly about individuals you met, available resources, or other aspects of the interview that left you with a favorable impression. As you draw the letter to a close, mention your understanding

Seven Ways to Ruin Your Cover Letter

1. Spell the company's name incorrectly.
2. Send the letter to the wrong address.
3. Address the letter "Dear sir" even when the hiring authority is a woman.
4. Misspell words and make typographical errors.
5. Use poor grammar.
6. Forget to enclose your résumé.
7. Omit your contact information.

of the next step in the hiring process and indicate your willingness to provide any additional information. In addition, you may wish to send a personalized thank you note or electronic message to the individuals involved with your interview.

Even if you do not want to pursue the position, you should still send a polite letter of thanks. Thank the person for the opportunity to interview for the position, and request that they withdraw your application from further consideration.

Declining an Interview

Sometimes you might send an application for a position or initiate a request for an interview (perhaps by sending a letter of inquiry), but your priorities change before an interview is confirmed. If you no longer want to pursue the position, send the interviewer a polite letter requesting that he or she withdraw your application. This notification displays your professionalism. Even if you have already indicated in a phone call that you no longer want the position, a letter makes it official and eliminates potential confusion between you and the interviewer.

Cover Letter Essentials

In the first paragraph, explain your reason for writing and tell the reader how you learned about the organization. When responding to a position announcement, state where you saw it.

In the second paragraph, specify key ways that your skills and background suit the position. Point out specific experiences or accomplishments that underscore your suitability for the job. Try to identify a unique attribute that makes you stand out as a candidate. Do not repeat the exact wording of your résumé or curriculum vitae. Use this section of the letter to elaborate on your key qualifications and how they meet the employer's needs. Refer the reader to your résumé for more information. If necessary, this section can take up two paragraphs.

In the closing paragraph, express your interest in the position and request an interview.

Postponing a Decision

If you need extra time to make up your mind about accepting a position, discuss it over the phone with the employer and follow up with a letter or electronic message. Begin by expressing your continued interest in the position and your appreciation for receiving an offer. Then state your need to postpone your decision. You can decide whether to include the specific reason you need additional time. Some possible reasons include evaluating other offers, assessing the compensation package, or discussing the pros and cons of relocating with your family. In the letter, give the recipient the date when you will provide a decision. In the conclusion, note your appreciation for the employers' cooperation and understanding. It is important to note that additional time to make your decision may not be granted, because the request can be interpreted as an indication of disinterest.

Declining a Position Offer

If you cannot accept a position, send a letter declining the offer as soon as you reach your final decision. If appropriate, you can state your reason for declining the offer, but it is not necessary. Include a polite closing statement expressing your appreciation for the organization's consideration.

Accepting a Position Offer

In your acceptance letter, sound gracious, professional, and enthusiastic. State that you accept the offer and appreciate the opportunity to become part of the company or organization. Confirm your official start date and other relevant details. Conclude the letter with an expression of thanks.

Preparing Letters

When you write cover letters and other correspondence related to pharmacy opportunities, always use a standard business letter style. You can find good books in your local library or bookstore that describe the business letter format.

The most commonly used business letter styles include the block, modified block, and modified semi-block formats. Figures 9.1, 9.2, and 9.3 are examples of these styles.[1] Health professionals routinely use the block style.

Try to write in a positive tone and use the active voice as much as possible (see sidebar "Use the Active Voice" on page 99). Pay attention to the details in your letter and proofread it carefully for spelling, typing, punctuation, and grammatical errors.

Elements of a Standard Letter

Letterhead

Before preparing your letters, create a standard letterhead containing your name and address. You can also include your telephone number and e-mail address. Usually, the

FIGURE 9.1 Block letter.

Actual size is 8.5 × 11 inches.

FIGURE 9.2 Modified block letter.

Actual size is 8.5 × 11 inches.

FIGURE 9.3 Modified semi-block letter.

Actual size is 8.5 × 11 inches.

Tip: Before you seal the envelope and mail your letter, proofread the contents again. Remember that your cover letter must create a positive impression to help advance you to the next level of evaluation.

letterhead is centered at the top of the page. For electronic communications, however, you may want to place the letterhead flush with the left margin to avoid a formatting conflict.

Margins

In all business letters, set the left, right, top, and bottom margins at one inch or greater.

Dateline

Type the dateline approximately three lines below the last line of the letterhead. You can insert additional space depending on the letter's length.

In the dateline, note the month, day, and year (e.g., July 24, 2017). Make sure to place a comma between the day and year. A style variation that is often used in government-related communications begins with the day in numeral form followed by the month and year (e.g., 24 July 2017).

In block-style letters, place the dateline flush with the left margin. In modified block or modified semi-block letters, place it to the right of the page's center.

Recipient Address

You can precede the recipient's name with a courtesy title (e.g., Dr., Mr., Ms.) unless an abbreviation of the recipient's degree follows the name. Do not put both a courtesy title and a degree. List the recipient's title and name as it appears on correspondence you have received from the person. Make sure you spell everything correctly.

If you cannot identify the contact's name, list the name of the department or unit within the organization, followed by the standard mailing address, city, state, and zip code. Verify the accuracy of the five- or nine-digit ZIP code by checking the United States Postal Service's website at http://tools.usps.com/go/ZipLookupAction_input.

Salutation

Type the letter's salutation two lines below the last line of the recipient's address and flush with the left margin. Follow the salutation with a colon.

Avoid using the impersonal introductions of "Dear Sir or Madam" or "Dear Director of Pharmacy." Reserve these generic salutations for times when you have exhausted all reasonable approaches for finding the name of the specific contact person. It is usually easy to call the organization and ask for the contact's name, title, and correct spelling.

Body

The body of the letter begins two lines below the salutation. Single space each line within a paragraph. Between paragraphs, use a double space. In block and modified block letters, keep all lines of each paragraph flush with the left margin. For modified semi-block letters, indent the initial line of each paragraph 5 to 10 spaces.

The first paragraph of the letter indicates your interest in the position and states how you learned about it. The second paragraph highlights your qualifications and experience and also notes how they match the position requirements. In this paragraph, you should also refer the reader to your résumé or curriculum vitae for additional details. The final paragraph mentions your willingness to arrange an interview and thanks the contact person for considering you for the position.

If your letter exceeds one page, begin the second page with a heading (flush with the left margin) that includes the name of the person receiving the letter, the date, and the page number.

Complimentary Close

Place the complimentary close two lines after the end of the body. In a block letter, the complimentary close appears flush with the left margin. In a modified block or semi-block

Use the Active Voice

The active voice is more direct, emphatic, and vigorous than the passive voice. In the active voice, the subject of the sentence does the action: George Washington chopped down the cherry tree. In the passive voice, the subject receives the action: the cherry tree was chopped down by George Washington.

Besides being boring, the passive voice can leave out important details. For example, if you say "Savings were gained from improvements in operations," the reader has no idea who made the improvements or brought about the savings. You can use the passive voice occasionally—if, for example, it does not matter who performed the action—but use it sparingly.

Tip: For best results, print your letter on quality paper using a laser printer. Never use wrinkled or torn paper. You can use an ink jet printer if it produces high-quality results, but do not use dot matrix printers.

letter, align the closing text under the dateline. Capitalize only the first letter of the complimentary close, and insert a comma at the end. You can choose your preferred complimentary close from the following examples typically used in business correspondence:

- Respectfully
- Respectfully yours
- Very truly yours
- Best regards
- Most sincerely
- Sincerely
- Sincerely yours

Signature Block

Type the signature block approximately four lines beneath and aligned with the complimentary close. Spell your name as it appears in your formal signature and letterhead.

Enclosures

Place a notation that acknowledges any enclosures flush with the left margin. You can use the word "Enclosure" or an abbreviation such as "Encl." If you have several enclosures, put the specific number before the "Enclosure" notation, or note it afterwards in parentheses. You can follow the notation with a colon and a brief description of the enclosure.

The Envelope

Envelope Size

Although most people routinely use an envelope with the dimensions $4\frac{1}{8} \times 9\frac{1}{2}$ inches (a #10 commercial envelope) for mailing letters, consider using an envelope that measures 9×12 inches. Larger and roomier, this size envelope is less likely to put noticeable creases in your cover letter and résumé or curriculum vitae, and it may stand out in the recipient's stack of mail.

Return Address

Place your name and return address—identical to the information that appears in your letterhead—in the upper left quadrant of the envelope. Figure 9.4 shows the placement of F4
a return address on a standard business envelope.

Recipient Address

When addressing an envelope, always use the same address information contained in the letter. The addressee's name and address should begin at the approximate center of the envelope. Common word-processing software will prepare a postal-approved bar code for the ZIP code (5 digit or ZIP+4).

FIGURE 9.4 Business envelope.

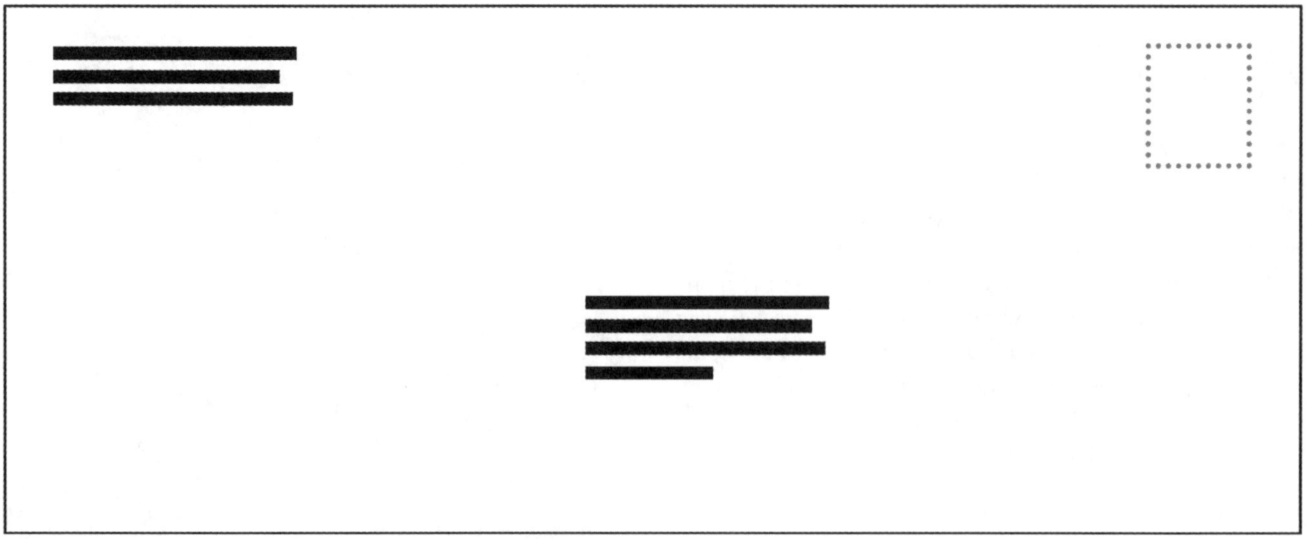

Actual size is 4.125 × 9.5 inches.

Tip: If you want to include a special mailing notation (e.g., "Certified Mail," "Registered Mail," "Personal," "Confidential") on your letter, capitalize the text, as shown, and place it approximately four lines below the dateline, flush with the left margin. Put the same notation on the envelope roughly four spaces above the first line of the addressee's name.

If desired, you can select this function when preparing the addressee's mailing address.

Special Notations

Place special mailing notations approximately four spaces above the first line of the addressee's name. Type these notations in all capital letters. The special notations "Personal" and "Confidential" are usually placed to the upper left of the addressee's name, whereas "Certified," "Registered," or "Special Delivery" are placed to the upper right.

Tip: If you are requested to or decide to submit an electronic copy of a letter or any documents as attachments, do not incorporate them in the body of the electronic message. Instead, prepare files of the documents and attach them to a brief electronic message.

Reference

1. Lindsell-Roberts S, Stevens MA. In: *Merriam Webster's Secretarial Handbook*. 3rd ed. Springfield, MA: Merriam-Webster; 1993:244–89.

CHAPTER 10

Tips, Checklists, and Sample Letters

This chapter provides sample letters to give you an idea of effective formats and wording. The letters serve various purposes, including responding to job announcements, seeking applications, confirming interviews, inquiring about internships, and expressing thanks. Just like the sample résumés and curricula vitae (CVs) in this book, the letters provided are only examples. You must tailor your letters to your individual needs and circumstances.

When you draft a letter, use the following guidelines to help you prepare final copy that meets professional standards.

Guidelines for Letter Format

- Adhere to customary business letter style and format.
- Use a standard letterhead containing your name and address.
- Include your telephone number as part of your standard letterhead. Otherwise, make sure to include it in the body of the letter.
- Place your letterhead symmetrically at the top of the page.
- Follow a consistent letter style (i.e., block, modified block, modified semi-block).
- Set all margins at one inch or greater.
- For block letters, type the dateline approximately three lines below the last line of the letterhead and flush with the left margin. For modified block or modified semi-block letters, put the dateline right of center or flush with the right margin.
- Place special mailing notations such as "Certified Mail," "Registered Mail," "Personal," or "Confidential" in capital letters approximately four lines below the dateline, flush with the left margin.
- In the inside address, include the name and address of the receiver followed by the standard mailing address, city, state, and ZIP code.
- Type the letter's salutation two lines beneath the last line of the inside address and flush with the left margin.
- Follow the salutation by a colon.
- In the body of the letter, use single-spaced paragraphs, with a double space between each paragraph.
- In block and modified block letters, keep the lines of each paragraph flush left. In modified semi-block letters, indent the initial line of each paragraph 5 to 10 spaces.
- Use the active voice and a positive tone throughout your letter.
- Review the content of your letter for spelling, typing, punctuation, and grammatical errors.
- If the content of your letter exceeds one page, begin the second page with a heading that includes the

Cover Letters with Résumés

The cover letter you send with your résumé or CV allows you to highlight special skills, share relevant personal information, and emphasize the benefits you can provide the employer or organization. Always present yourself in a positive light and follow these rules:

- State the position you are applying for.
- Summarize your qualifications.
- Describe how you can meet the organization's needs and what you can accomplish for the organization. Employers are far more interested in what you can do for them than in the benefits you seek.
- Show some knowledge of the company or institution by weaving in accurate details.
- Sound polite, yet confident.
- Mention that your résumé is enclosed and indicate your desire to meet with the employer.

name of the person receiving the letter, the date, and the page number.
- Place the complimentary close two lines after the last line of the letter's body. In a block letter, keep it flush with the left margin. In a modified or semi-modified block letter, align the complimentary close under the dateline.
- Capitalize only the first letter of the complimentary close, and place a comma at the end.
- Type the signature block approximately four lines beneath, and aligned with, the complimentary close.
- If you use a notation (e.g., "Enclosure" or "Encl.") to acknowledge additional items in the envelope, type it flush with the left margin. You may follow the notation with a colon and a brief description of the enclosure.
- Print the final letter using quality paper and a laser printer. Try to use paper of the same quality as your résumé or CV.

Tips on Writing Letters

Chapter 9 highlighted types of letters and standard formats to aid you in preparing professional correspondence. But what about the writing itself? When composing a letter, your goal is always to communicate clearly. Good writing is simple, which means it reads well, is easy to follow, and does not contain unnecessary words. Even complex ideas can be expressed with short words and succinct paragraphs.

Many people in business and academia are used to reading documents choked with clutter. The sentences are overly complicated and full of extra-long words and redundant phrases. It is difficult to determine what the writer is trying to say. But seeing how common such writing is, people think they must imitate this inflated style to sound intelligent and fit in with their chosen community. Here are a few communication techniques to remember:

- Be brief and to the point.
- State your purpose in the first paragraph. This will focus your reader and keep his or her attention.
- Use a natural tone in your writing. Do not try to sound like someone you are not. Of course you must use good grammar and the right level of formality for your audience—no slang or off-color words—but avoid sounding fake or pretentious.
- Never use long words when short words work well. For example, instead of "facilitate" say "help" or "ease." Instead of "numerous" say "many."
- Prune excess words. Unnecessary words slow the reader and smother your message. A sentence is wordy if it can be tightened without loss of meaning. Table 10.1 gives examples of wordy phrases and how to condense them.
- Do not smother verbs. Sometimes excellent verbs are smothered in sentences, because they are presented as nouns. For example, instead of saying "make a decision" it is more effective to say "decide." Instead of "establish a connection" say "connect."
- Use clichés sparingly or not at all. Clichés are trite, overused expressions, such as "light as a feather" or "hit the nail on the head." Whenever you are tempted to use a cliché, ask yourself if there is a more effective way to make your point.
- Review, revise, and polish after you write your first draft. No one crafts a perfect letter in the first attempt. If the stakes are high—such as applying for a position you really want—do not ruin your chances with sloppy, unclear writing.

TABLE 10.1 Examples of Simplified Wordy Phrases

Wordy Phrase	Condensed Phrase
Be considered that	Is
Despite the fact that	Although
Exhibits the ability to	Can
For the purpose of	For
In light of the fact that	Because
In the event that	If
In the final analysis	Finally
In the proximity of	Near
It is obvious that	Obviously
On an annual basis	Yearly
On an everyday basis	Routinely
On the occasion of	When
Start off	Start
Subsequent to	Later

LETTER 1 Lauren G. Smith

This cover letter in response to a job announcement for a pharmacy technician is positive, clear, and direct.
Font: Times New Roman 12 point.

Lauren G. Smith

4501 Canyon Boulevard • Ogden, Utah 84403 • (801) 621-9469

May 15, 2017

Pamela Davis, R.Ph.
Davidson's Pharmacy
210 W. 200 South
Salt Lake City, Utah 84120

Dear Ms. Davis:

This letter is in response to your announcement of a pharmacy technician position opening in the May 14th edition of the *Salt Lake Tribune.*

I am looking for such a position to gain experience in a community pharmacy setting in the Salt Lake City area. While most of my experience has been in the inpatient setting at Great Canyon Hospital, I have eight months of recent experience working in the hospital's ambulatory care clinic pharmacy. A copy of my resume is enclosed.

I will contact you during the next week to arrange a convenient time to meet. Thank you in advance for considering my request.

Sincerely,

Lauren G. Smith

Enclosure

Note how she emphasizes her strengths.

It is good that she shows initiative here; she should be sure to follow through and make contact, as promised.

Actual letter size is 8.5 × 11 inches.

LETTER 2 Danielle Shaffer

A short, readable request for an application to a Doctor of Pharmacy program.
Font: Arial 12 point.

Danielle Shaffer
1201 Ryan Street
New Castle, Pennsylvania 16105

August 22, 2016

It would be better to include a contact name, especially since the writer is serious enough about this school to request a meeting.

Office of Admissions
School of Pharmacy
University of Pittsburgh
1104 Salk Hall
Pittsburgh, Pennsylvania 15266

Dear Director of Admissions:

I am currently completing my prerequisite courses for the Doctor of Pharmacy degree at Gettysburg College.

Would you please send me an application for admission to your program, beginning in the Fall of 2017. In addition, I would like to meet with you to review my academic plan and arrange a tour of your campus.

I can be reached by voice mail at (717) 258-4473 or by e-mail at deshaffer@netlink.com. Thank you for accommodating my request.

Sincerely,

Danielle Shaffer

Actual letter size is 8.5 × 11 inches.

LETTER 3 Monica N. Sims

This request for an application to a nontraditional Doctor of Pharmacy program is businesslike and to the point.
Font: Georgia 12 point.

Monica N. Sims, R.Ph.
7453 Sunset Circle
St. Louis, Missouri 63123

It is helpful to include full contact information, including telephone number and e-mail address.

March 10, 2016

Director of Admissions
School of Pharmacy and Allied Health Professions
Creighton University
2200 Nebraska Plaza
Omaha, Nebraska 68348-0545

Addressing this letter to a specific person would be more effective.

Dear Director:

After five years of pharmacy practice, I am interested in changing my career path. Would you please send me an application for admission to your nontraditional Doctor of Pharmacy program.

I look forward to your response.

Sincerely,

Monica N. Sims

Actual letter size is 8.5 × 11 inches.

LETTER 4 Lorraine M. Meyer

This inquiry about internship openings provides clear details and good information to "sell" the candidate.
Font: Georgia 12 point.

Lorraine M. Meyer

7225 Pine Tree Place
Omaha, Nebraska 68116

Telephone: 402. 431.9664
E-mail: lmm387@neb.edu

January 15, 2017

Kimberly Ferguson
Albertsons Inc.
General Offices
460 Sumpterfield Drive
Boise, Idaho 83682

Dear Ms. Ferguson:

I am completing the second year of a Doctor of Pharmacy degree at the University of Nebraska College of Pharmacy. My goal is to obtain a pharmacy internship during the summer of 2017.

Dr. Lindsey Elliott, my faculty mentor, has informed me that you may have internship openings in the Lincoln area. I will be returning to Lincoln at the completion of the academic year and will be available for employment from June 1 through August 15, 2011. I am registered as a pharmacy intern with the Nebraska Board of Pharmacy. A copy of my resume is enclosed for your review.

I would appreciate being considered for a position. Please use the contact information above to reach me at your earliest convenience.

Sincerely,

Lorraine M. Meyer

Encl.

After highlighting her interest in the internship and her background, she might consider adding a polite note that she will call the recipient next week.

Actual letter size is 8.5 × 11 inches.

LETTER 5 Grant D. Hayes

In requesting an interview at a residency showcase, this writer is succinct and courteous, but the letter could be better organized.
Font: Times New Roman 12 point.

Grant D. Hayes

1320 Sunset Place	Residence: (785) 865-9037
Lawrence, Kansas 660947	Cellular: (785) 334-8072
grant.hayes@zipnet.com	Fax: (785) 865-9054

November 24, 2016

Michael A. Strickland, Pharm.D.
Pharmacy Residency Program Director
Department of Pharmacy
Thomas Jefferson University Hospital
141 South 10th Street
Philadelphia, Pennsylvania 19107-5098

Dear Dr. Strickland:

I am presently completing the final year of a doctor of pharmacy degree at the University of Kansas School of Pharmacy. I have ten years of pharmacy practice experience, as a pharmacy technician in the United States Navy and more recently as a pharmacy intern at the University of Kansas Medical Center.

My career goal is to practice in a health-system pharmacy. In achieving this goal, I plan to pursue a pharmacy practice residency. I will be attending the ASHP Midyear Clinical Meeting in Orlando, Florida next month. I hope to speak with you about your program at the Residency Showcase. If you have any information that can be provided before the ASHP meeting, I would appreciate receiving a copy at the address above.

Again, I look forward to meeting you in Orlando to learn more about your residency program.

Sincerely,

Grant D. Hayes

> A busy reader might not continue further to realize that the writer is seeking more than written information. The writer could move the second sentence to the following paragraph.

> It would be better for the writer to state in the first paragraph that he is seeking a meeting at the showcase so the recipient immediately understands the letter's intent.

> To ensure a meeting, the writer should consider asking for a specific appointment and should say he will call to set one up, which shows initiative.

Actual letter size is 8.5 × 11 inches.

LETTER 6 Erin B. Rogers

A request for an application to a residency program.
Font: CG Omega 12 point.

Erin B. Rogers
8559 Hunter Drive
Memphis, Tennessee 38118
901.547.8995
ebrogers@silvernet.com

October 18, 2016

Rodney J. Harrison, Pharm.D.
University of California at San Francisco
521 Parnasus Avenue, Room A 194
San Francisco, California 94143-0608

Dear Dr. Harrison:

In the first paragraph, it is helpful to state the reason for writing. She could move her interests and qualifications to the second paragraph.

I am currently completing a pharmacy practice residency program at the Regional Medical Center in Memphis. During my residency and Doctor of Pharmacy program, I have gained experience in working with oncology patients. I enjoy the challenges of this patient population and plan to pursue a specialized residency in oncology pharmacy practice.

I have enclosed my curriculum vitae for your review. I would appreciate receiving an application for your residency program. I plan to attend the upcoming meetings of the American College of Clinical Pharmacy (ACCP) and the American Society of Health-System Pharmacists (ASHP). I would appreciate the opportunity to meet with you to discuss my qualifications and the possibility of pursuing your specialized residency.

During the next week, I will contact your office to see if I can arrange a brief session with you at either the ACCP or ASHP meeting. Thank you in advance for considering my request.

Sincerely,

Erin B. Rogers

Enclosure

Actual letter size is 8.5 × 11 inches.

LETTER 7 David K. Reed

A cover letter inquiring about a drug information fellowship that does a good job of getting right to the point.
Font: Century Gothic 12 point.

DAVID K. REED

4416 Hawthorne Place
Philadelphia, Pennsylvania 219131

(215) 879-5135
dkreed32@usip.edu

November 14, 2016

Brenda A. Miller, Pharm.D.
Associate Professor of Pharmacy
Rutgers, the State University of New Jersey
College of Pharmacy
242 Frelinguysen Road
Piscataway, New Jersey 08855-0634

The font is a bit difficult to read.

Dear Dr. Miller:

I anticipate graduating with a Doctor of Pharmacy degree in May 2017 from the Philadelphia College of Pharmacy at the University of the Sciences in Philadelphia. During the past three years, I have been able to gain experience in the area of drug information services through my internships and clerkships. My advisor, Dr. Julia Narducci, has recommended I contact you about the drug information fellowship offered jointly by your college and Bristol-Myers Squibb.

I have enclosed a copy of my curriculum vitae and three writing samples of drug information monographs I have prepared for the Presbyterian Hospital's Department of Pharmacy Services. I would welcome the opportunity to meet with you to discuss your fellowship. If you would kindly contact me at the address I have provided, I will be pleased to schedule an appointment at your convenience.

The way he highlights an area of particular interest is nice.

Sincerely,

David K. Reed

Enclosure

Actual letter size is 8.5 × 11 inches.

LETTER 8 Alexis Seay

A cover letter in response to an ad for a hospital pharmacist.
Font: Times New Roman 12 point.

ALEXIS SEAY

8602 Kenyon Boulevard
Seattle, Washington 98136
(206) 923-6813
amseay@landnet.com

June 2, 2016

Judith Jennings
Department of Human Resources
Denali Center/Fairbanks Hospital
3570 Landover Street
Fairbanks, Alaska 99605

Dear Ms. Jennings:

I am responding to your recent advertisement in *Pharmacy Today* for a staff pharmacist with infusion therapy experience. I am a recent graduate of the University of Washington School of Pharmacy with part-time employment experience at Home Infusion Services, Inc. in Seattle. A copy of my curriculum vitae is attached.

As a native of Alaska, I have an interest in relocating to the Fairbanks area. I would appreciate arranging an appointment to discuss the details of this position. I will be in the Seattle area until June 15th and can be contacted at the above address. I plan to return to return to Alaska by June 22nd. After this date, my address will be: 110 Caribou Circle, Big Delta, Alaska 99736. I will be able to be reached by telephone at (907) 457-3188 and my e-mail address will remain unchanged.

If possible, I would like to arrange an interview when your schedule permits. Thank you in advance for considering my request.

Sincerely,

Alexis Seay, Pharm.D.

Enclosure

> The typographical error in this paragraph is a problem, suggesting to the reader that the writer does not pay attention to detail. Careful proofreading is essential.

> Although her request for an interview is courteous, the approach is passive, leaving it up to the interviewer to take the initiative.

Actual letter size is 8.5 × 11 inches.

LETTER 9 Allison Kay Wells

A concise, effective cover letter that follows up on a phone inquiry about a position.
Font: Arial 12 point.

Allison Kay Wells, Pharm.D., M.B.A.

4726 Preston Drive
Dallas, Texas 75240
(972) 239-1875
akwells@aol.com

April 2, 2016

Note that she writes the same day as the conversation, reinforcing her interest.

Suzanne Harrison
Blue Cross Blue Shield of Massachusetts
300 Newton Street
Boston, Massachusetts 02114

Dear Ms. Harrison:

As we discussed this morning, my family and I are planning to move to the Boston area within the next two months. I have four years of experience in developing and managing the clinical programs associated with pharmacy benefit management plans. I would like to explore the opportunities of a similar position at Blue Cross Blue Shield of Massachusetts.

I am enclosing a copy of my curriculum vitae for your review. I understand that you may have an opening in the near future and I would appreciate your consideration in contacting me to arrange an interview.

Sincerely,

Allison Kay Wells, Pharm.D., M.B.A.

Enclosure: Curriculum vitae

Actual letter size is 8.5 × 11 inches.

LETTER 10 Austin D. Walker

A gracious request for a letter of reference.
Font: Verdana 12 point.

Austin D. Walker

5028 Highland Park Drive
Milwaukee, Wisconsin 53217

414-352-4225
adwalker@aol.com

January 12, 2017

James R. Rutherford, Ph.D.
Professor, Pharmaceutical Sciences
School of Pharmacy
University of Wisconsin
425 N. Charter Street
Madison, Wisconsin 53706-1584

It is helpful that the writer provides a stamped envelope and lets the recipient know the deadline.

Dear Dr. Rutherford:

I enjoyed our brief telephone conversation this afternoon and I appreciate your words of encouragement concerning my interest in pursing graduate studies.

I have enclosed a copy of my curriculum vitae and the reference form requested by the Office of Graduate Admissions at the University of Texas. Also, an addressed and stamped envelope is included for your convenience. The deadline for submitting my completed application is March 1, 2017.

I will keep you informed about the status of my admission. Again, I appreciate the time and effort to complete a reference on my behalf.

Best regards,

Austin D. Walker

Actual letter size is 8.5 × 11 inches.

LETTER 11 Janette L. Walker

Cover letter in response to an announcement about an assistant professor position.
Font: Georgia 12 point.

Janette L. Walker, Pharm.D.

8716 Fuller Drive
Albany, New York 12206

(518) 432-7384
jlwalker@empirenet.com

July 9, 2016

> She should note how her experience will benefit the school if she is hired, that is, what is special about her qualifications and experience, and how do they match the needs of the position.

John H. Turner, Pharm.D.
Professor and Chair
Department of Pharmacy Practice
State University of New York at Buffalo
Amherst, New York 14180

Dear Dr. Turner:

I have enclosed a copy of my curriculum vitae in response to a recent announcement in the *AACP Report* for an assistant professor position at your school of pharmacy.

I believe my current faculty experience in ambulatory care could be beneficial to your academic programs. My qualifications and experience are consistent with the position description in the announcement. Additionally, the opportunity to pursue a tenure track position is appealing.

I would welcome an invitation to meet with you to discuss the position in greater detail. I may be reached at the above address.

Thank you for your consideration.

Sincerely,

> Her closing is passive and does not demonstrate initiative.

> It is nice that tenure track appeals to her, but this fact will not sell the employer on her as a candidate. It is more important to use this space to emphasize her strengths.

Janette L. Walker, Pharm.D.

Enclosure: Curriculum vitae

Actual letter size is 8.5 × 11 inches.

LETTER 12 Courtney K. Moore

A courteous, readable acceptance letter for a position.
Font: Verdana 12 point.

Courtney K. Moore, Pharm.D.

3664 Salem Boulevard ▪ Elizabeth, New Jersey 07206 ▪ 908.965.3108

June 12, 2016

A professional, concise, readable letter.

Brian J. Sheridan, Pharm.D.
Director of Operations
HLM Managed Care, Inc.
1835 Carlton Pike
Cherry Hill, New Jersey 08036

Dear Dr. Sheridan:

This letter will serve as my formal acceptance of your offer to join HLM Managed Care, Inc. as a clinical account manager. The conditions of employment outlined in your letter of June 4, 2016 are acceptable to me.

As requested, I will contact the Human Resources Division to complete all required application information.

I have tendered my resignation with my current employer, effective July 15, 2016. I will be able to meet the August 1, 2016 start date specified in your letter.

Again, thank you for providing me with this unique opportunity. I look forward to working with you and the other members of your department.

Best regards,

Courtney K. Moore, Pharm.D.

Actual letter size is 8.5 × 11 inches.

LETTER 13 Louisa C. Morales

A request to be withdrawn from consideration for a position.
Font: Century Schoolbook 12 point.

Louisa C. Morales, Pharm.D.

513 Lynnhurst Terrace
Los Angeles, California 90043

Telephone: (323) 293-2342
E-mail:lcmorales@cedarnet.com

March 12, 2016

This polite letter leaves a good impression, which is a plus should the writer and recipient cross paths again.

Lauren Patterson, Pharm.D.
Clinical Coordinator
Department of Pharmacy
University of California
Irvine Medical Center
218 South Medical Drive
Orange, California 92558

Dear Dr. Patterson:

Thank you for the opportunity to meet with you to discuss your clinical pharmacist position opening. I appreciate the courtesy you and your staff extended during my informative visit.

As we discussed during the interview, I am attempting to balance my personal and professional goals in seeking a position. Based on my inability to accommodate a rotating schedule, I ask that you withdraw my candidacy from further consideration.

I was impressed with your organization and know that I would enjoy being a member of your staff. You have my best wishes for a successful search.

Sincerely,

Louisa C. Morales, Pharm.D.

Actual letter size is 8.5 × 11 inches.

LETTER 14 Jonathan H. Elliott

A request for withdrawal of an application.
Font: CG Times 12 point.

Jonathan H. Elliott, Pharm.D.
4840 Naylor Drive
Washington, D.C. 20009
(202) 483-9664
jonathan.elliott@horizon.com

March 15, 2016

Even when you are not interested in a position after applying, it is important to convey a positive attitude, as this writer does.

Tricia E. Hall, Director
Department of Pharmacy
St. Elizabeth Medical Center
4300 East Avenue
Bridgeport, Connecticut 06604

Dear Ms. Hall:

Thank you for the opportunity to meet with you and your staff to discuss my qualifications in filling a clinical coordinator position. I appreciate the courtesy and hospitality you extended during my stay in Bridgeport.

After thoughtful consideration, I ask that you withdraw my application from further consideration. My decision is primarily based on the inability of my spouse to relocate at this time.

Again, thank you for the time you spent informing me about your impressive organization.

Sincerely,

Jonathan H. Elliott, Pharm.D.

Actual letter size is 8.5 × 11 inches.

LETTER 15 Tyler R. Owens

A letter confirming the time and date for an interview and noting that a CV is enclosed.
Font: Arial 12 point.

Tyler R. Owens, R.Ph.

2410 Willow Drive • Chesapeake, VA 23322 • 757.482.5993 • trowens@erols.com

May 25, 2016

This letter says exactly what it needs to, and no more.

Francis L. Wood, Pharm.D.
Director of Pharmacy Services
Albright Medical Center
Victoria, Virginia 23184

Dear Dr. Wood:

Thank you for providing me with an opportunity to interview with you and your staff on Monday, May 31st at 9:00 a.m. in your office. A copy of my curriculum vitae is attached. Please let me know if you need additional information about my qualifications and experience. I appreciate your consideration and will look forward to meeting you.

Sincerely,

Tyler R. Owens, R.Ph.

Encl.

Actual letter size is 8.5 × 11 inches.

LETTER 16 Matthew D. Briggs

A thank you letter following an interview.
Font: Lucida Bright 12 point.

Matthew D. Briggs, M.S., R.Ph.

7045 Cooper Drive
Columbus, Georgia 31907
(706) 563-4226
mdbriggs@aol.com

April 16, 2016

Note the nice way he emphasizes his interest in the position.

Matthew K. Blake, Pharm.D.
Syncor
3712 Barrow Street
Nashville, Tennessee 37205

Dear Dr. Blake:

Thank you for providing me with an opportunity to interview with you and your staff. I appreciate the time and effort you spent in organizing this informative session.

My interview convinced me that I would like to work as a member of your staff. I have a definite interest in pursuing the nuclear pharmacist position. Please let me know if you need additional information about my qualifications or experience. I will look forward to hearing from you.

Sincerely,

Matthew D. Briggs, M.S., R.Ph.

Actual letter size is 8.5 × 11 inches.

LETTER 17 Tracey N. Jennings

A letter declining an interview for a residency.
Font: Times New Roman 14.

Tracey N. Jennings
1424 Lewis Street
Boston, Massachusetts 02114

February 4, 2017

Lia Chang, Pharm.D.
Pharmacy Residency Program Director
Veterans Affairs Medical Center
84 Oak Street
Rochester, New York 14738

> In declining an interview, this writer's tone is gracious, and she gives a clear reason without belaboring it.

Dear Dr. Chang:

I want to thank you for inviting me to interview for your pharmacy practice residency. After reassessing my career goals, I have decided to seek employment rather than a residency position in the coming year. You have my best wishes for a successful search.

Sincerely,

Tracey N. Jennings

Actual letter size is 8.5 × 11 inches.

LETTER 18 Laura K. Ross

A thank you letter following an interview.
Font: Garamond 14 point.

Laura K. Ross, R.Ph.

9640 Pine Street
Providence, Rhode Island 02907
(401) 785-8968
lkross@zipnet.com

August 14, 2016

Shelly Peterson, R.Ph.
Recruitment Director
CVS Corporation
1 CVS Drive
Woonsocket, Rhode Island 02836

> The writer misses an opportunity here to reiterate her career interests and emphasize how her strengths will benefit the organization.

Dear Ms. Peterson:

Thank you for the opportunity to interview with you and your colleagues yesterday. The goals of your organization are consistent with my career interests. I left with a positive impression.

My interview convinced me that I would like to work with your organization. I have a definite interest in pursuing the position and look forward to hearing from you soon.

Sincerely,

Laura K. Ross, R.Ph.

Actual letter size is 8.5 × 11 inches.

LETTER 19 Courtney K. Moore

Thank you letter to a person who served as a reference.
Font: Verdana 12 point.

Courtney K. Moore, Pharm.D.

3664 Salem Boulevard ▪ Elizabeth, New Jersey 07206 ▪ 908.965.3108

June 12, 2016

Madhu N. Mehta, Pharm.D.
Assistant Professor of Pharmacy
Rutgers, the State University of New Jersey
College of Pharmacy
242 Frelinguysen Road
Piscataway, New Jersey 08855-0634

It is very thoughtful to let the reference know how the job search turned out.

Dear Dr. Mehta:

I am pleased to inform you that I received and accepted an offer of employment with HLM Managed Care, Inc. in Cherry Hill as a clinical account manager. I will begin my new position on August 1, 2016.

I appreciate all of your assistance during the past several months in serving as a reference and helping me evaluate the merits of different offers.

Again, thank you for all you have done to advance my career.

Sincerely,

Courtney K. Moore, Pharm.D.

Actual letter size is 8.5 × 11 inches.

LETTER 20 Mark A. Williamson

A letter that follows up on an interview and serves as a cover letter for a portfolio CD-ROM.
Font: Univers 14 point.

Mark A. Williamson
2581 Courtland Terrace, Kokomo, IN 47802
(765) 868-6504 mawilli3@purdue.edu

January 25, 2016

Calling the recipient's attention to the letter's subject can be useful when you are following up on a previous meeting or interaction.

Ruth G. Harrison, M.S.
Director of Pharmacy Services
Montgomery Regional Hospital
2105 Rosewood Boulevard
Montgomery, AL 36116

Re: Resident Match Number 13579

Dear Mrs. Harrison:

Please accept my thanks for extending an invitation to interview for your pharmacy practice residency program. I appreciate the time that you and your staff devoted to me during the day-long interview session.

I am convinced that I would like to complete a pharmacy practice residency under your guidance. The enclosed CD-ROM contains my portfolio, which provides additional information about my educational accomplishments and professional practice development during the past six years. Please let me know if you or your staff need any additional information prior to concluding the residency match process.

Sincerely,

Mark A. Williamson

Actual letter size is 8.5 × 11 inches.

Presenting a Professional Image

CHAPTER 11

Whenever you meet someone new, that person forms a first impression of you within seconds. Good or bad, these impressions last a long time.

As a pharmacy professional, you must remain aware of your professional image at all times. Your appearance, communications (written, verbal, nonverbal), and manners represent major components of your professional image.

This chapter gives an overview of professionalism that you can use as a framework for guiding and enhancing your professional development. The chapter then covers two major obstacles to presenting a professional image during interviews and other encounters—nonverbal communication and dining etiquette—and includes tips for succeeding in these areas.

Professionalism

You demonstrate your professionalism each day by the way you look, think, and act. Throughout your career, your professional reputation will be one of your biggest assets, opening doors and providing opportunities in a way that nothing else can—not a perfect résumé, prestigious education, or impressive employment history.

Pharmacists' ethical traits—a key component of professionalism—are rated so highly in annual surveys that they serve as a model for all members of the health care community. For more than 20 years, pharmacists have scored at or near the top when Gallup surveys the public about how it perceives the ethics and honesty of key professions.

Members of the pharmacy profession embody the concept of "professionalism" by sharing many common characteristics, according to a white paper on pharmacy student professionalism published in 2001.[1] In addition to knowledge and skills, these traits include trustworthiness, accountability, ethically sound decision making, and leadership. The following sections provide an overview of the professional traits expected of you as a pharmacist.

Knowledge and Skills

Pharmacy professionals display knowledge and competence in their unique areas of expertise. They follow professional norms and behaviors. They communicate effectively and use critical thinking to solve problems.

Commitment to Self-Improvement

Pharmacy professionals accept and respond to constructive feedback and seek opportunities for improvement. They recognize their limitations and seek assistance when necessary. They continually seek to improve their knowledge and skills throughout their lifetime.

Service Orientation/Altruism

Pharmacy professionals serve others. They provide service to their community and do not seek to profit unfairly from others. They put the needs of the patients they serve above their own.

Pride in the Profession

Pharmacy professionals demonstrate a strong work ethic and commitment to the profession. They are loyal, conscientious,

Nonverbal Cues

- Make direct eye contact, especially at the time of an introduction.
- A sincere smile conveys confidence and a positive outlook. Remember that a negative facial expression can easily negate a positive message.
- Members of the profession usually shake hands upon meeting. Give a firm hand shake with two short shakes. Practice shaking hands with colleagues to perfect the skill.

Professional Dress for Women

- Professional dress for women often begins with a comfortable suit in a conservative color such as black, blue, brown, or beige accompanied by a tailored blouse in a contrasting solid color or muted print.
- Conservative pumps or flats should be considered good shoe choices, especially since many interview sessions involve tours or walking to meet with various interviewers.
- Keep accessories such as jewelry, scarves, and hosiery conservative.
- Minimize or eliminate atypical body adornments such as multiple earrings in one or both ears. Consider masking any tattoos, if possible.
- Keep your makeup muted and avoid strong fragrances.
- Keep your nails clean and preferably short. Use only muted colored nail polish.
- Carry a small attaché or portfolio along with your purse, if necessary.

and well prepared. They attempt to exceed expectations and strive for excellence.

Covenantal Relationship with Patients

Pharmacy professionals display compassion and empathy to patients and other caregivers. They respect patients' privacy as well as their diversity of race, gender, religion, sexual orientation, age, disability, and socioeconomic status. They take time to explain information to patients and serve as advocates for those who cannot advocate for themselves.

Creativity and Innovation

Pharmacy professionals participate in activities that contribute to developing new knowledge and practice. They embrace change and apply creative and innovative approaches to challenges.

Accountability

Pharmacy professionals demonstrate initiative, reliability, and follow through in fulfilling their commitments. They meet deadlines and complete their responsibilities in a timely manner. They accept responsibility for their errors and control their emotions appropriately, even under stressful conditions.

Ethically Sound Decision Making

Pharmacy professionals display honesty and forthrightness when they interact with patients, peers, faculty, and other health professionals. They adhere to high ethical and moral standards. They cope with life's situations despite the high degree of complexity and uncertainty these events entail.

Leadership

Pharmacy professionals contribute to the profession and actively participate in professional organizations. They take a proactive role in solving social issues by providing leadership in their community. They help build and maintain a culture that promotes professionalism.

Professional Presence

Members of the pharmacy profession have high professional expectations of their colleagues. As a result, you need to focus on your professional presence when seeking a pharmacy-related position. Professional presence has to do with hard-to-define social abilities and manners. In addition, emotional intelligence creates the capacity to be aware of, control, and express one's emotions, and to handle interpersonal relationships in a judicious and empathetic manner. When someone has a professional demeanor, it inspires confidence in others and makes them feel good about the person's abilities. Bottom line—a good professional presence means creating a positive impression.

Begin by focusing on your nonverbal communication, including your eye contact, facial expressions, handshakes, and professional attire. Nonverbal communication is so powerful that even when you are saying one thing, people may interpret something else from your tone of voice or body language.

The first three sidebars in this chapter contain important tips to remember about nonverbal communication. No matter how flamboyant or offbeat you like to be with your looks and behavior during "down time," the safest—and most professional—route is conservative.

Professionalism in an Electronic Environment

The pervasiveness of electronic technology in today's pharmacy practice settings may induce pharmacists to become cavalier about their professional behavior in an electronic environment, especially when using the internet and social networks.

As a pharmacist, your image online should reflect the image of a health care professional. You should routinely search the internet by typing your name in any of the usual internet search engines, such as Google, Yahoo, or Bing, and reviewing the available information. If you maintain the usual electronic networking sites such as Facebook and LinkedIn and your profile settings allow public view, an entry should be available at the time of an internet search. This easy access can be beneficial for individuals seeking to network with you, but it can be a liability if your profile contains any information that could be construed as unprofessional.

Although participation in social media networking such as Facebook, Twitter, Instagram, blogs, and YouTube is primarily for personal use, it is important to remember that there is no total separation of your public life and your personal life in an electronic environment. Employers, program directors, colleagues, and others will likely use the information on social networking sites to make judgments about your character. Review all your social media sites and eliminate any wall posts, images, groups, or fan pages that could be interpreted as controversial or unprofessional. You should also check the profiles of your friends on a regular basis to monitor pictures and comments that are posted about you. Do not assume that your profile can be viewed only by your friends even when you have established strict privacy settings.

Always use caution in posting content and images on your online social networking sites, personal webpages, and blogs. Avoid stating personal views about your employer, faculty, administrators, and colleagues. Keep your blog posts, tweets, and updates objective and professional.

Professional Dress for Men

- Professional dress for men usually begins with a pure wool or wool blend suit. Common colors include dark gray or dark blue, with or without a subtle pinstripe pattern. Make sure your coat sleeves end at the middle of your wrist bone. You can have your pants finished with either a cuffed or plain bottom.
- Wear a long-sleeved, light-colored dress shirt with a darker tie.
- Common types of ties include solid color silk ties or those with repeating patterns of geometric prints or stripes. Make sure your tie complements your suit.
- Properly knot your tie using a four-in-hand, Windsor, or half-Windsor knot. Your tie should hang down to the center of your belt buckle. You do not need to use a tie clip or pin. Avoid clip-on ties, unless you have a physical disability that limits your manual dexterity.
- Your dark leather belt and oxford style shoes should match in color.
- Wear freshly polished shoes.
- The color of your socks should match your shoes or your pants. Choose a conservative color and pattern. When in doubt, choose a solid black sock.
- Minimize or eliminate atypical body adornments such as earrings in one or both ears. Consider masking any tattoos.
- Keep your hair style conservative and trim any facial hair.
- Carry a small attaché or portfolio, if necessary.

Dining Etiquette

Most interview sessions involve one or more meals. As a result, you need to understand and follow established rules of dining etiquette. It may seem trivial, but proper etiquette for eating plays a significant role in making a good impression. That said, if you are unsure exactly what to do at some part of the meal, try to relax. Do what strikes you as logical and gracious.

Unfortunately, many interviewers do not wait for the conclusion of a meal to begin questioning applicants. This means that you will do most of the talking while the interviewer or interviewers savor their meal. Answering their questions takes top priority, so do not worry about finishing your food.

Most of your conversation will relate to pharmacy during an interview session or other discussion, although you may venture into small talk as well. Do not lose sight of good manners, no matter how enthusiastic you feel as the conversation turns to the Red Sox, One Republic, or Brad Pitt. Knowing and applying appropriate social behavior remains imperative for a successful interview.

The following guidelines should help you appear confident and comfortable at any meal function.

Beginning the Meal

- Turn your cell phone off before arriving at the restaurant. Never answer your cell phone at the table.
- Leave your purse or attaché or other items under your chair.
- Place your napkin on your lap, either after your host does so or when handed to you by a server.
- Select a medium-priced entrée.
- When everyone at the table has been served, follow the lead of your host to begin eating.

Table Manners

Using good table manners helps create a positive impression in an interview. The list below contains basic—but very important—table manners for you to follow.

- Do not chew food with your mouth open.
- Do not talk with your mouth full.
- Keep your elbows away from the table surface by eating with one hand and placing the other on your lap.
- Avoid seasoning your food before tasting it.
- Do not chew ice.
- Do not pour coffee or tea from your saucer into your cup.
- Chew and swallow your food before taking a drink of any liquid.
- Say "no, thank you" to the wait staff instead of turning your cup or wine glass over if you do not want coffee or wine.
- Always ask others to pass items to you rather than reaching across the table.
- Pass food and other items to the right.
- Pass the salt and pepper together.
- Pass the gravy or salad dressing vessel with the handle of the ladle facing the receiving individual.
- Ask for a replacement if you drop your flatware or napkin.
- Do not use a toothpick to clean your teeth.

During the Meal

- If you leave the table during the meal, put your napkin on the seat of your chair or to the left of your plate.
- Avoid sharing food, even if offered.
- Use discretion in drinking alcoholic beverages.
- Do not smoke at the table, even if you are in a smoking section of a restaurant.
- Avoid complaining about the food or service.

Special Protocol

The Place Setting

The place setting will vary with the formality of the meal. In general, a place setting consists of a plate in the center with forks, napkin, and bread and butter plate on the left. A knife, teaspoon, soup spoon, glasses for water and wine, and cup and saucer are positioned to the right. You may find a dessert fork and spoon at the top of the dinner plate. Figure 11.1 shows the typical place setting.

It is amazing how many people are confused about the use of each plate and utensil. Typically you start with those on the outside and work your way inward. When in doubt about how to proceed, observe your host or take cues from others at the table.

Foods to Avoid

- Avoid making an issue about your special dietary needs (e.g., allergies, religious observances, vegetarian), because most restaurants have a variety of food choices.
- Consider saying "no, thank you" when offered soup, especially if you have a tendency to spill food.
- Avoid pasta that has long strands, such as spaghetti or linguine.

Utensils

- At the beginning of the meal, select flatware farthest from the plate and work inward as the meal progresses.
- Use your fork and knife in the American style by holding the knife in your right hand and fork in your left hand with the fork tines piercing the food. After cutting a bite-size portion of food, lay your knife across the top edge of your plate with the sharp edge facing you. Change the fork to your right hand with the fork tines facing up. Figure 11.2 provides a visual example.
- Use your knife—not your fingers—to push food onto your fork.
- Using your knife, cut one bite-size portion of food at a time.
- Use your knife and salad fork to cut any large piece of salad just prior to eating.
- Never return a used piece of flatware to the table top.

Bread Plate

- Place a pat or two of butter on your bread plate, and pass the butter to the person on your right before attempting to butter your bread.
- Remember that your bread plate stays on the left and liquids go on the right side of your plate. Servers remember this as solids on the left and liquids on the right.
- If the person to your left uses your bread plate by mistake, ask the server for another plate.
- Break a small portion of your bread, and butter the portion prior to eating it, rather than cutting or buttering all your bread at one time.

FIGURE 11.1 **Typical place setting.**

A. Dinner Plate
B. Soup Bowl
C. Bread Plate
D. Napkin
E. Salad Fork
F. Dinner Fork
G. Dinner Knife
H. Teaspoon
I. Soup Spoon
J. Butter Knife
K. Dessert Fork
L. Dessert Spoon
M. Water Glass
N. Wine Glass (Red)
O. Wine Glass (White)
P. Coffee/Tea Cup and Saucer

FIGURE 11.2 **American style for holding a fork.**

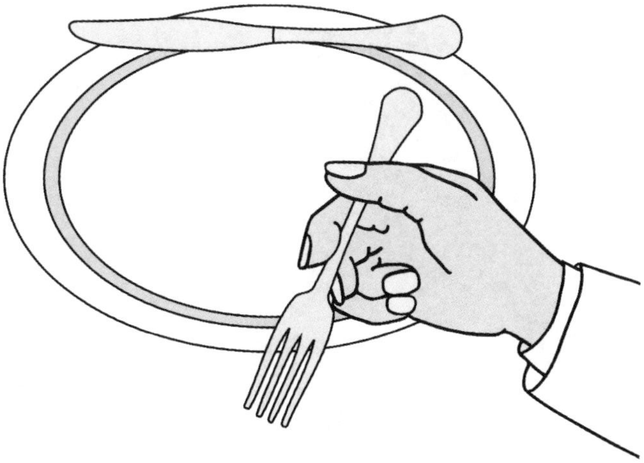

Soup

- When eating soup, dip the spoon in the soup and push the spoon away from you rather than toward you before lifting the spoon to your mouth.
- Do not slurp when eating your soup or blow on hot soup.
- Do not leave your spoon in a cup or bowl. Instead, place it on the side of the saucer or plate beneath the bowl.

Finishing the Meal

- You do not need to eat everything on your plate, especially if you are responding to multiple questions from interviewers.
- At the completion of your meal, visualize your plate as the face of a clock. Leave the knife (blade facing inward) and fork (tines down) with the sharp ends of each pointing toward 10 and the flat ends pointing toward 4 (see Figure 11.3). This configuration lets the server know you are done.

FIGURE 11.3 Position of utensils after completion of meal.

- Do not move your plate when you finish and do not stack plates for the server.
- When you finish your meal, place your napkin on either side of your plate, although the right side is considered most acceptable. If a waiter has removed the plate, place your napkin in the center of the plate area. Do not place your napkin on your plate.
- Do not request a doggy bag for any unfinished food.

Reference

1. Anon. White paper on pharmacy student professionalism. *J Am Pharm Assoc.* 2000;40:96–102.

Introduction to Searching and Interviewing

CHAPTER 12

The old saying "You get only one chance to make a good first impression" conveys why it is critical to prepare for the interview process. Interviews give you the opportunity to communicate your knowledge, skills, abilities, and interests to potential employers, admissions personnel at educational institutions, and others in a position to make decisions that affect your future. With so much hanging on one interaction, you do not want to wing it.

Interviews allow job candidates and employers to assess the suitability of a match. You get the opportunity to highlight your knowledge, skills, abilities, and interests and to gather useful information about the employer or institution.

Interviews also give you a chance to gather information about an employer or institution. Basically, they provide a way for both parties to determine the suitability of a match.

To make the most of your interview, you need to do your homework. First, ferret out the most worthwhile opportunities for you. Then ready yourself for interviews that cast your strengths in the best possible light and tell you what you need to know about the potential employer. Chapter 13 provides more extensive information on preparing for an interview.

Your Personal Marketing Materials

Before beginning your search, update all the documents you plan to use. Proofread all your documents—from your business card through your portfolio—to ensure current, consistent, and accurate information.

When seeking a position, you may need to use a combination of materials. Figure 12.1 shows some of the tools you might use during your search and interview process.

Routinely, you will need a letter of introduction and a résumé or curriculum vitae. You may also want to prepare an elementary presentation portfolio consisting of your business card, career statement, and curriculum vitae. In addition, you can create a cover letter that includes a link to your electronic portfolio.

The personal marketing documents you decide to use should depend on the situation. Too much information in an initial contact may overwhelm a potential employer. Instead, use an incremental approach. For example, you can use a cover letter and curriculum vitae for introductory purposes. At the time of an interview, you might provide an elementary presentation portfolio or a copy of your portfolio on a flash drive accompanied by your business card. You might consider preparing an elevator speech, that is, a clear, brief message about you. It should communicate who you are, what you are looking for, and how you can benefit a company or organization. The message typically takes about 30 seconds to read, the time it takes people to ride from the top to the bottom of a building in an elevator.

Requesting References

Selecting which references to use depends on the type of position you seek. Some employers or program directors will ask you to provide a set number of references, whereas others will indicate specific numbers and types of references. When providing references, keep the following points in mind:

- Give careful thought to the position description, and attempt to match prospective references with the type of position.
- Contact your references ahead of time, or meet with them personally to explain the potential position and its importance to you.
- Provide each reference person with a copy of your résumé, curriculum vitae, or portfolio to ensure

Preparing a Business Card

A business card is a convenient and inexpensive marketing tool. When you meet decision makers at networking events, educational sessions, and conferences, presenting them with your business card in a courteous, professional way may help to fix your name in their mind.

Your card should be clean and professional. The standard dimensions of 2 × 3.5 inches require that you be selective in your wording and design so that the card is not overcrowded. The usual type size varies from 8 point to 11 point; the key is to make sure it is readable. If you work for a corporation or organization, it may specify the images and color that must be used. Otherwise, keep the card simple by using black ink on 100-pound professional white, off-white, or cream card stock. A horizontal format is most common for health professionals, as shown on the samples.

Common information for your business card includes

- Name
- Title
- Organization's street address
- Alternative or home mailing address
- City and state abbreviation
- ZIP + four mailing code
- Telephone number
- Alternative or mobile telephone number
- Fax number
- E-mail address
- (Optional) Social media address (e.g., LinkedIn, Twitter)

You can store the same information in a Microsoft Outlook contact record and then create a Vcard that can be e-mailed as an attachment. You can also store the information in your personal digital assistant (PDA) or Smartphone to create an electronic business card. This file allows you to quickly beam your contact information to another person who has a similar device equipped with an infrared port. Some PDAs and handheld devices cannot communicate with other brands, so you may choose to install software on your device to eliminate electronic transfer problems.

FIGURE 12.1 Continuum of personal marketing materials.

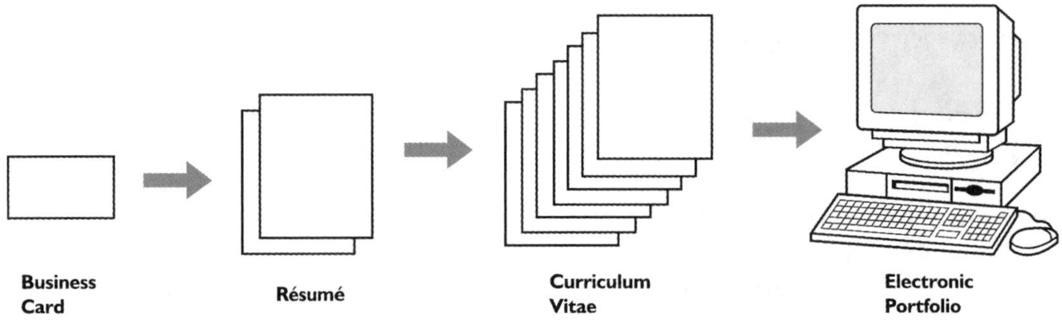

the accuracy of any details they might include in a reference letter. Also include a copy of the position description or other specifics about the potential position.

- Some reference forms may give you the option to waive your right to future access to the recommendation letter. Waiving this right shows employers you have trust and confidence in the recommender.
- Some employers, residency programs, or graduate programs may provide a standardized form as part of a reference request. Review the individual components (e.g., oral and written communication skills, leadership, intellectual ability, reliability, judgment, interpersonal skills, adaptability, ethical behavior, professional appearance) of the form prior to selecting your references.
- In some cases, potential employers will contact references directly. Make certain that you list the current contact information for your references, especially telephone numbers and e-mail addresses.
- At the completion of the process, send a thank you note to those who prepared references and tell them of your search outcome.

Search Techniques

Networking

The network of contacts you have established throughout your life can provide invaluable help in your search process. Key contacts include friends and acquaintances you interact with in your daily activities as well as people you know through past or current employment. Other valuable sources are faculty and classmates you met during education or training classes. People you meet through organizational activities, especially those connected to the pharmacy profession, can also help.

In the pharmacy profession, personal networks typically bring much better results than traditional means in helping people find opportunities that fit well with their interests and strengths. For example, a mentor may know about a new position that has yet to be advertised. Or a colleague may connect you with his or her network of associates in another geographic area.

Put the word out to your peers and mentors—people you trust and respect—that you are exploring a job change or seeking a specific kind of opportunity. Even if they have no suggestions at the moment, they can serve as sounding boards and be on the look out for useful possibilities.

Depending on your immediate need, you will want to have a definite objective when meeting with a contact in your network. For example, if you have been terminated from your current position, you can discuss your situation and explain what happened, ask for help, and seek strategies for gaining a new position and possible contacts. The need for follow-up and a thank you note should not be overlooked.

Advertisements

To some extent, the approach you follow for finding potential jobs depends on the type of position you seek. One common strategy involves reviewing advertisements on the internet, and in newspapers, professional newsletters, and journals. Because of the time delay associated with print media, however, only routine staff positions are announced this way. Because newspaper readership soars on Sundays, it is the best day of the week to check the employment section for positions in the health professions. Some employers prefer to target newspapers with the greatest circulation within a state or region, so do not rely on your hometown paper alone.

Advertisements in newsletters and journals published by professional organizations generally have the greatest time delay. As a result, they are not the best way for employers to announce entry-level positions they need to fill quickly. Because newsletters and journals have an extensive and focused readership, they are useful for announcing nationwide searches for management and specialist positions and for highlighting positions that have remained vacant for a long time.

Plenty of other sources for printed job announcements exist, including flyers and listings at pharmacy schools. Schools and colleges often help employers announce positions to students and alumni. Usually, the dean's office or alumni staff can provide this information to students.

Placement Services

Many state and national pharmacy organizations offer placement services. These services vary from merely posting available positions for attendees to review (common at state meetings) to linking employers and applicants through a more structured process (more typically found at national meetings). Placement services at professional meetings routinely connect prospective graduate students, residents, and fellows with programs in their area of interest.

State and national organizations often maintain electronic databases of prospective employers and applicants, usually as a membership service or for an additional fee. Most likely, pharmacy organizations' placement services, such as the American Pharmacists Association's Career Center, can best meet your needs, because they have the clout and visibility to attract listings from top employers.

Career Day Events

Career day events are a popular way to recruit new graduates for employment or postgraduate training. Most schools and colleges hold such forums once a year. Similar to the placement services at state and national meetings, prospective employers visit the campus to interview graduating students for internships and employment. These visits provide a great opportunity for students seeking local and regional opportunities. Typically, you can sign up a few days in advance or that day for on-site interviews with representatives from various companies and organizations.

The Internet

The internet offers an unsurpassed announcement method because of the immediacy of position listings, around-the-clock search availability, and convenience. Opportunities posted on the internet commonly are announced through other communication channels, but the internet gives you a quick, easy way to find a wealth of choices.

Some general sites promote health professional recruitment for many disciplines. Other sites tend to focus on specific employers or specific types of positions. Table 12.1 provides a sample listing of internet sites.

Because the internet constantly changes, some of these addresses may become invalid. You can find other useful sites by keying the type of employment you desire into popular search engines, such as Google.

TABLE 12.1 Internet Sources for Position Listings

Organization	URL
American Association of Colleges of Pharmacy	http://www.aacp.org
American College of Clinical Pharmacy	http://www.accp.com
American Pharmacists Association	http://www.pharmacist.com
American Society of Consultant Pharmacists	http://www.ascp.com
American Society of Health-System Pharmacists	http://www.ashp.org
Bio Careers	http://www.biocareers.com
BioSpace	http://www.hirehealth.com
Career Innovation	http://www.careerinnovation.com
Career Mosaic	http://www.careermosaic.org
CareerBuilder	http://www.careerbuilder.com
Chase Group, Inc.	http://www.chasegroup.com
Chem Jobs	http://www.chemjobs.net
CollegeGrad.com	http://www.collegegrad.com
GradSchools.com	http://www.gradschools.com
Graduate Guide	http://www.graduateguide.com
HealthcareSource	http://www.HealthcareSource.com
Job-Hunt	http://job-hunt.org
Jobvertise	http://www.jobvertise.com
LifeScienceJobs.com	http://www.lifesciencejobs.com
MedOptions.com	http://www.medoptions.com
Monster Healthcare	http://healthcare.monster.com
National Association of Chain Drug Stores	http://www.nacds.org
Petersons	http://www.petersons.com
PharmacistJobs.com	http://pharmacistjobs.com
Pharmacy Technician Certification Board	http://www.ptcb.org
PharmacyWeek	http://pweek.com
Pharmstaff, Ltd.	http://www.pharmstaff.com
RPh on the Go	http://www.rphonthego.com
Rx Career Center	http://rxcareercenter.com
SHS, Inc.	http://www.shsinc.com
United States Air Force	http://hp.airforce.com
United States Army	http://www.army.mil
United States Food and Drug Administration	http://www.fda.gov
United States Navy	http://www.navy.com
United States Pharmacopeia	http://www.usp.org
United States Public Health Service	http://www.usphs.gov
University of Oklahoma School of Pharmacy	http://www.pharmacy.ouhsc.edu

If a particular company or institution interests you, visit its website to obtain information about employment opportunities. Most web pages have an easily identified icon indicating the link to position openings. In addition, visit the company's official LinkedIn page, Facebook page, Twitter account, and blog. Social and business networks are a convenient way to learn more about the organization that you may be considering as an employer.

The use of a business network website such as LinkedIn may also be considered. LinkedIn offers several avenues for exploring position opportunities. You can indicate that you are interested in career opportunities and will accept messages from other LinkedIn members. Groups and companies will allow you to explore collections of specific groups such as a professional organization or national employers. By examining specific groups or companies, you will be able to see various LinkedIn individuals associated with these entities. A quick review of their rosters may reveal individuals known to you or individuals you will want to contact about potential position openings. LinkedIn also maintains a "Job" menu that has an extensive search feature.

Professional Recruiters

Professional recruiters serve as intermediaries between employers and prospective employees. Most recruiters get paid by the employer after filling a specific position. Firms accepting contingency fees receive payment only when an individual is hired.

Some recruiters arrange a direct fee-for-service agreement with the prospective employee. Most of the time you probably can find worthwhile opportunities without using a recruitment firm, but this route may make sense if you seek an upper-level management position or need to relocate to a geographic area where you do not have a professional network in place.

In general, a recruiter focuses on locating an applicant who meets the exact qualifications specified by an employer, rather than attempting to find the ideal position for you. Look for a reputable recruitment firm with a long-standing record. Before signing a contract, ask for references—a list of pharmacists you can contact who have used the service. Avoid signing any agreement that limits you to one recruitment agency. Make certain that the recruiter does not edit your resume or curriculum vitae without your permission and approval. You should consider whether you want to retain prior approval for the recruiter to send any information about you to a prospective employer. Before arranging an interview, determine that the position described by the recruiter is consistent with your qualifications and expectations. You might also consider asking the firm to send you a copy of its code of ethics.

Interview Basics

Doing Your Research

Before going on an interview, you need to learn as much as you can about the company or institution. Manuals on interviewing always tell you to evaluate your strengths and weaknesses beforehand so that you can effectively promote your assets. Similarly, you should review the strengths and weaknesses of the potential employers you have identified in your search process. Gather annual reports, company brochures, newspaper and magazine articles, information from the company websites, and material about the company posted on other websites.

The internet as well as the career counseling staff or reference librarian at your local or college library may be helpful in providing information on prospective employers. Read the material carefully. Note the facts presented, the questions raised, the positive aspects revealed, and any concerns that arise in your mind. With this information in hand, you can prepare targeted questions for your interview.

Invitations to Interview

Employers usually do not invite you for an interview until you have provided sufficient background information, such as a fully completed application form and résumé or curriculum vitae. In large corporations, your information may be scanned electronically for keywords and screened by several people. In small companies, maybe only one or two people will sort through it.

Depending on the organization's size and recruitment strategy, a limited number of applicants will be invited for an interview. Most organizations handle invitations by telephone so that they can arrange a mutually convenient appointment. Organizations usually make these calls during working hours, so remember to provide a telephone number at which prospective employers can reach you during the day. If you can receive calls only at home, make sure you have an answering machine or voice mail.

Screening Interviews

Potential employers commonly conduct initial screening interviews to identify the most promising candidates. In some organizations, staff from the human resources department, rather than pharmacy personnel, handle the interviews. The screening interview usually lasts no longer than 30 minutes. The interviewer focuses on specific criteria to determine whether your knowledge and skills meet the position's requirements. He or she will also convey background information about the organization and position. To gain a second interview, you need to project a positive image and present qualifications that fit well with the available position.

Finding Residencies and Fellowships

For information about available positions for graduate students, residents, or fellows, you usually need to go directly to the sponsoring institution. Most maintain a website to describe their program offerings and admission requirements. If you need help identifying programs, you can obtain a list of offerings from professional organizations such as those listed here.

Academy of Managed Care Pharmacy
675 North Washington Street, Suite 220
Alexandria, VA 22314
http://www.amcp.org
(703) 684-2600

American Association of Colleges of Pharmacy
1727 King St.
Alexandria, VA 22314
http://www.aacp.org
(703) 739-2330

American Association of Pharmaceutical Scientists
2107 Wilson Blvd., Suite 700
Arlington, VA 22201
http://www.aaps.org
(703) 243-2800

American College of Clinical Pharmacy
13000 W. 87th Street Parkway
Lenexa, KS 66215-4530
http://www.accp.com
(913) 492-3311

American Pharmacists Association
2215 Constitution Avenue, NW
Washington, DC 20037-2985
http://www.pharmacist.com
(202) 628-4410

American Society of Consultant Pharmacists
1321 Duke St.
Alexandria, VA 22314
http://www.ascp.com
(800) 355-2727
(703) 739-1300

American Society of Health-System Pharmacists
4500 East-West Highway, Suite 900
Bethesda, MD 20814
https://www.ashp.org
(866) 279-0681

National Association of Chain Drug Stores
1776 Wilson Boulevard
Arlington, VA 22209
http://www.nacds.org
(703) 549-3001

National Community Pharmacists Association
100 Daingerfield Rd.
Alexandria, VA 22314
http://www.ncpanet.org
(703) 683-8200

The National Pharmaceutical Association
107 Kilmayne Dr., Suite C
Cary, NC 27511
www.npha.net
(877) 215-2091

Quite often, screening interviews are conducted by telephone. Although impersonal, this approach offers an efficient and cost-effective solution, especially when long distances exist between you and the interviewer.

Sometimes screening interviews are recorded on video. You might meet with a designated third party who will ask you a list of prepared questions and send the completed video file to the interviewer.

Potential employers may also ask you to go to a convenient site that has teleconferencing equipment, such as a local college or a business hotel, where they can interview you over a video monitor. The use of electronic interactive interviews is used routinely by some employers and program directors. You can communicate and answer questions over the internet using a software application such as Skype or Facetime.

Selection Interviews

The second interview, often considered a selection interview, is usually conducted by personnel with the authority to extend an offer if they decide you best fit the position. The interview may be one-on-one, a group meeting, or a combination of both. Some last a few hours; others take an entire day. During the session, interviewers will seek more information about your knowledge, skills, and professional experience. The interviewer may rely on specific questions pertaining to the position, or the interview may take the form of a casual conversation. The latter style encourages

Six Major Interview Formats

An interview can take many different formats. By preparing yourself for these different possibilities, you will gain a much stronger edge in the interview process.

1. *Behavioral Interview*. This type of interview looks at your past performance as a predictor of future success. Interviewers will ask open-ended questions to identify your problem-solving skills, accomplishments, and areas for improvement. They will also seek specifics about past events and your role in the events. This method of interviewing attempts to get responses to actual, not hypothetical, situations.

   Ideally, you should respond to a situation-based question using a story about your actual experience. Expect a series of follow-up questions, such as What did you do next? How did you feel? What was your role? What were you thinking? What was the result? In this type of interview, you must demonstrate actual results from your acquired experiences.

2. *Stress Interview*. In this approach, the interviewer typically uses intimidating verbal and nonverbal communications such as maintaining long periods of silence, avoiding eye contact, and challenging your comments in an aggressive or unfriendly way. The interviewer may even misinterpret your response to evoke a counter response. This kind of interview highlights when and how you assert yourself. Although not a common style of interviewing, you can succeed with this type of approach if you do not take the interviewer's behavior personally.

3. *Group Interview*. Some organizations include several interviewers in a room with a single candidate—or several candidates together. Although applicants tend to find group interviews stressful, they can help employers determine how you interact outside of one-on-one situations.

   In one type of group interview, interviewers will represent different personality characteristics, such as friendly, arrogant, and assertive. They then evaluate you on how well you handle the various styles while responding to specific questions. Another approach uses the peers you would work closely with—if hired—as the interviewers.

4. *Directive Interview*. This type of interview requires the interviewer to ask each candidate the same series of predetermined questions. The questions usually align with the specific tasks and duties of the position description. Although a rigid process, this type of interview gives you an opportunity to provide additional information when responding to each specific question.

5. *Case Study*. Yet another tack involves gathering several applicants in a room and having them complete a task or evaluate a case study. For example, the interviewer might ask you to design a therapeutic regimen for a patient with several chronic diseases or determine the best means of reducing prescription waiting time at a hypothetical pharmacy. As the group reviews the case study, conflicting views emerge and the interviewer assesses the applicants' styles in terms of problem solving, decision making, creativity, and the ability to work effectively on a team.

6. *Luncheon or Dinner Interview*. This type of interview assesses your performance in a social situation and gives interviewers the opportunity to continue with their evaluation of you as a prospect. Because this type of interview is often very intimidating, Chapter 11 includes tips for making the situation successful. Remember that some employers may use other social venues such as meetings or receptions to assess your social behavior.

The Thank You Note

Always follow up your interview with a thank you note for both screening and selection interviews. In the case of a group interview, send a thank you note to everyone you met with—or at least to the primary interviewers.

Interviewers appreciate these notes, which not only demonstrate good manners but also help remind interviewers who you are and what you offer. Sometimes a thank you note provides the extra something that makes you stand out from the crowd. For a personalized touch, write your note by hand using your best penmanship. Although popular, electronic messages are not the ideal way to send a personal thank you note.

An effective thank you note should

- Remind the interviewer of the position you desire.
- Stress your interest in the position and the company.
- Emphasize one or two of your strongest skills, tailored to the interviewer's concerns.
- Include your contact information and the best times to reach you.
- Close with a suggestion for further action, such as a second meeting.
- Be brief—roughly a dozen sentences.
- Be free of spelling errors, typographical errors, and other gaffes.

Do not let the note backfire on you by begging for the position or coming across as if you think you already have the job.

open communication and allows you to steer the discussion toward your strengths.

The sidebar on the previous page details specific formats that interviewers may use to assess your qualifications and personal style.

Following the Interview

After the interview, prepare a personal summary of new information you learned during the session. In your notes, include perceptions of people you met, details about the environment, and facts about the position. Although you may think you will remember clearly everything you saw and heard, memories fade. After several interviews, details from one site can be confused with those from another. Also, make sure you record the names of your interviewers, especially if they did not provide an itinerary.

Write a thank you note as soon as possible after the interview, preferably the same day. Address it to the primary interviewer, and include the names of any people you found especially helpful during the interview session. Keep the note positive and highlight your continued interest in the position.

CHAPTER 13

The Interview: Before, During, and After

Preparing for the Interview

Do Your Homework

Learning as much as you can about an organization before an interview will help you make the most of your time during the session. You will come across as thorough, professional, and highly interested in the position. Advance preparation also enables you to ask better questions, so you are more likely to obtain the information you need to evaluate the position.

To obtain background information, you can request it directly from the company during your preliminary discussions. The World Wide Web provides another excellent source. Use any common search engine to locate the company's web address. Once you have found the website, look for the following information about the company:

- Location
- Type of facilities
- Organizational structure
- Reputation
- Personnel demographics
- Scope of products or services provided
- Mission
- Vision
- Values
- Strategic plan
- Financial position

You can find financial information in annual reports, public records, and on the internet. In the case of for-profit corporations, stock brokerage firms can provide financial history information. Online financial news periodicals and investment directories have excellent information and also provide links to other helpful sites.

Look for evidence of the company's financial viability. Important things to know include whether the company plans to expand, the company has soaring or plummeting stock value, or another company seeks to acquire it.

You can also search other sites and online publications for information about the company. For example, a magazine profile or newspaper articles can provide insights into a company's strengths, philosophy, future directions, and so on. Electronic resources such as LexisNexis—which may be accessible through your local library or university—can retrieve recent articles that give you a sense of the company's focus and direction.

If you know any current or past employees of the companies of interest, they can be an additional source of information. Ask them about the work atmosphere, and look for insights into the organization's strengths and weaknesses. Remember, however, that their perspectives are subjective and limited to their own experiences. Round out your research with input from other sources so you are not relying strictly on one person's opinion.

Fill Out Application Forms

Before extending an interview invitation, many organizations require that you complete an application form. Remember the following important points.

Provide Details

Follow instructions carefully and pay attention to detail as you fill out the form. Although your curriculum vitae (CV) should contain most of the requested general information, resist the temptation to complete blanks by stating "see attached curriculum vitae." The application needs to stand on its own in case it becomes separated from the CV. For example, some offices file applications in one place and CVs and background materials in another. Some scan applications and store the information electronically.

Filling out the application completely also conveys a message that you work thoroughly and conscientiously—and that you care enough about the position to do things correctly.

List Employment History

Applications will ask for the beginning and ending dates of past employment. If requested, list your employment dates and provide a brief statement explaining your reason for leaving. Try to cast your comments in a positive light, such

E-mail Etiquette

Electronic messages have become an increasingly important part of interview communications. As a result, you must make sure your e-mail messages portray a professional image at all times. When drafting e-mail messages, remember these tips.

Do

- Try to reply to e-mail messages in the same time period that you would return a telephone message.
- Use the same proper grammar, spelling, paragraph structure, and punctuation that you would for other written communications.
- Choose a subject line that accurately reflects your reason for communicating. Make it descriptive, such as "confirming our meeting tomorrow," instead of a label such as "meeting."
- Set the text wrap feature (via the preferences option on your e-mail tool bar) at approximately 75 characters.
- Save your message in draft form and put it aside to review again before you send it. People tend to dash off e-mails quickly, which invites errors, so take the time to proofread carefully. If you receive a message that evokes an emotional response, such as anger or frustration, do not respond immediately.
- Remember that e-mail messages are public and long-lasting documents. Write as if the whole world will read your message.
- Try to keep your message brief (e.g., less than a page in length). Use concise wording and stay on topic.
- Keep the tone of your message friendly and professional.
- If you attach documents to supplement your message, tell the reader what you have attached. Understand that some people may not open attachments because of fear of viruses.
- Prepare a proper signature with your complete contact information.

Don't

- Use emoticons (e.g., smiley faces) in professional communications.
- Use your personal e-mail address if the address does not sound professional (e.g., cutiepie@centralcom.net).
- Attach extensive documents unless you can convert them to PDF files.
- React immediately to flaming (unprofessional, emotional, rude) messages.
- Send personal information such as your Social Security number.
- Complete the "To" portion of the e-mail address until you have finalized your message, thus averting an unintentional "send."
- Mark every message as priority or urgent.
- Send repeat messages when you do not receive an immediate response to your initial message.

as "to gain additional practice experience" or "to return to college on a full-time basis." Avoid negative statements.

Give Salary History

Some applications will request your salary or wage history. Make sure you have starting and ending figures for each position. Some employers may request this information on a per-hour basis, whereas others may request the same information as an annual figure.

Occasionally, an application form may request your salary or wage expectation. In this case, ask colleagues about the organization's salary or wage structure. You can also get general information about salaries and wages by reviewing published advertisements that include salary ranges, talking with professional recruiters, and reviewing internet sites. Some sites list specific salary and wage information (e.g., https://www.bls.gov and http://www.pharmacyweek.org). Others enable you to determine appropriate salaries according to the cost of living in selected geographic areas (e.g., http://www.homefair.com). To avoid listing a specific amount on the application, you can simply use the word "negotiable."

Remember, Neatness and Spelling Count

Keep your application neat and avoid typographical or spelling errors. If you need more space, append a sheet and carefully cross-reference your responses. Print your responses by hand or—for the best results—type them. Or ask for a form that you can download from the internet and complete on your computer. Then you can either send the completed form electronically or print and mail a paper copy. You can also scan a paper application form and complete it on your computer.

Complete all sections of the application. Use the words "none" or "not applicable" for sections that do not apply to you. For concerns about how requested information such as date of birth, marital status, dependents, disabilities, arrests, and convictions will be used, talk with a representative of the nearest Equal Employment Opportunity Commission field office. Call 1-800-669-4000 to obtain the number of a specific field office, or check the website at https://www.eeoc.gov.

As a final step, review the application for completeness and accuracy. Sign and date it and make a copy for your files. Unless you complete the application on site, you may consider attaching a cover letter before you send the completed document.

Getting Ready

Practice, Practice, Practice

The interview gives you an opportunity to truly sell yourself. Review your résumé or CV, and practice responses to questions about your education, professional experience, and accomplishments. Review the position description, and create a mental list of your assets that meet these requirements. Chapter 14, "Sample Interview Questions," provides more detail on questions that interviewers frequently ask. Prepare scenarios or stories based on your experiences that you can use to answer situation-based questions. Make sure your comments do not sound too "rehearsed." Finally, think about tactful responses to inappropriate questions that inexperienced interviewers may ask you.

Conduct Mock Interviews

You may want to ask a colleague or mentor to conduct a mock interview to help you gain experience. Constructive feedback on your responses and delivery style can help you work out the kinks in advance. Student pharmacists often utilize the career services staff of their university or faculty members to conduct mock interviews.

Develop Question Lists

Most interviewers give you the opportunity to ask questions, so prepare a list of items you would like to learn more about. Keep your questions geared toward helping you understand your scope of duties and how you would fit into the organization. At a minimum, plan to ask three to five questions. Interviewers may become turned off by questions that seem irrelevant.

Remember Your Manners

It is a good idea to review books or articles on business etiquette and, if the interview involves lunch or dinner, table manners. You do not want to ruin a good impression by making a faux pas. Interviewers will look at both how you answer questions and how you conduct yourself overall.

Telephone Interview Tips

- Arrange a quiet and private space with ample time before, during, and after the interview so that you will not be interrupted.
- Ensure that you know whether you are to call the interviewer or the interviewer will contact you. Provide your correct area code and telephone number.
- If the interviewer requests a teleconference such as Skype or FaceTime, prepare your background surroundings in advance, dress as you would for an interview conducted on site, and look at the camera.
- Consider a photograph of a friendly individual or group of individuals, and pretend that you are speaking to the individual or individuals, rather than speaking to a blank wall or desktop.
- Ensure that you have water available.
- Conduct a mock interview with a colleague.
- Have a copy of your curriculum vitae available.
- Have a list of questions to ask.
- Use a land line telephone if available.
- Avoid using a speaker phone to reduce the chance of a lost connection.
- If using a cell phone, check your telephone signal strength and battery duration in advance.
- If using a headset, make certain the volume of your voice is reasonable by making a call to a colleague in advance.
- Initiate your call at the correct time, allowing for differences in various time zones.
- Speak in your normal voice (e.g., tone, pitch, pace, volume, inflection, articulation).
- Consider standing rather than sitting if you are not participating in a teleconference.
- Smile and be enthusiastic.
- Actively listen to the interviewer's question before responding.
- Make certain you know the name of your interviewer. The interviewer should introduce any other people listening to or participating in the interview session. Make a note of the name or names of the individuals.
- Be concise in answering a question, and limit the response to 1½ to 2 minutes to avoid monopolizing the discussion.
- Instead of typing your notes on a computer, take notes with a pen to avoid background noise of clicking keys.
- Have your calendar ready for scheduling an on site interview, if offered.
- Express your thanks for the opportunity to interview.
- It is usually acceptable to send an e-mail thank you note immediately following a telephone interview.

Participating in a Telephone Interview

A telephone interview may be your initial contact with a potential employer, because this is an efficient means of screening a large number of applicants. This type of interview does not permit the benefits of nonverbal communication skills, so you will need to conduct the interview in a quiet room, void of distractions. If the interviewer requests a teleconference such as Skype or FaceTime, plan to organize the background area in advance. It will be important to ensure that your telephone connection remains uncompromised for the duration of the interview. Because you will most likely use a cell phone, check your cell phone signal strength and battery duration in advance. If you foresee any problem with your cell phone, use a land line telephone. It is important to project a resonant voice. This is best achieved by communicating in a standing rather than a sitting position. A practice telephone call with a colleague asking sample interview questions can help you prepare for the experience.

During the interview session, try to avoid monopolizing the conversation. A general rule is to speak in increments of 1½ to 2 minutes. Make certain to have a calendar so you can check available dates and times for a personal interview. Consider a telephone interview as important as a face-to-face interview, and send a thank you note following the session.

Prepare for Presentations

Some interview sessions may call for a formal presentation. Residency and faculty candidates, for example, may be asked to deliver a seminar. If possible, consider asking the employer or program director about the audience, a general idea of their expectations, and the type of technology that will be available for your use. To ensure success in a formal presentation, make sure you prepare adequately. Rehearse in advance by arranging a presentation before colleagues and faculty so that you can receive constructive comments about the content and delivery of your presentation.

Dress for Success

Appearance and grooming remain important elements of a successful interview. Project a professional image by wearing a dark-colored, conservative suit. Usually, dark blue, black, and gray are good color choices. Men should wear freshly shined dress shoes, whereas women should wear low-heeled pumps or flats. Wear your hair in a neat and professional style. Avoid wearing perfume, cologne, or aftershave. Chapter 11 provides additional tips for projecting a professional image.

Responding to the Interview Invitation

When you are invited for an interview

- Write down the date, time, and location of your appointment.
- Request directions to the site.
- Record the name of your interview contact, and check how to pronounce his or her name.
- Ask for key details about the interview process, including duration and format.
- If applicable, request an interview itinerary. (Larger organizations and those proficient in conducting interviews usually provide an itinerary in advance.)

The Interview

Bring Applicable Documents

Bring along a slim briefcase, pad holder, or portfolio that contains a copy of your résumé or CV, business cards, one or more lists of your references, and questions you can review when you are not actively interviewing.

Arrive on Time

Interviewers like punctuality. Arrive 10 to 15 minutes before your scheduled appointment, allowing yourself time to relax and collect your thoughts. Your interview actually begins upon arrival. Be mindful of being courteous to the receptionist, and politely wait for your interview to begin. If the interview involves significant travel, allow as much extra time as possible to accommodate airline delays, lost luggage, jet lag, and other common annoyances associated with travel.

Use Nonverbal Communication Cues

From the outset, use appropriate nonverbal communication skills. Make eye contact, smile, and give the interviewer a firm handshake. Introduce yourself in a courteous manner. Avoid addressing your interviewers by first name unless they request otherwise. Do not sit down until the interviewer begins to sit or offers you a seat. Consider exchanging business cards: the information can be helpful in preparing thank you notes following your interview.

Maintain an enthusiastic and confident attitude at all times. Be alert and attentive—especially after lunch and during the late afternoon segment of a day-long interview, when energy tends to wane.

Remember Mealtime Etiquette

If your interview session includes a meal, pay particular attention to your dining etiquette. Choose your food carefully so that you can stay focused on your interviewer. Avoid anything that has a tendency to splatter or might easily lodge in your teeth, including a messy pasta dish or a thick sandwich dripping with sauce.

Do not think of the meal as a gourmet experience—it is business. Chapter 11 provides additional tips on dining etiquette.

Control Nervous Habits

Before your interview, ask friends or relatives if they have noticed that you have any nervous habits. Do you tend to chew on a fingernail? Lick your lips repeatedly? Twirl a lock of hair? Try to become conscious of anything you do that could be distracting or unprofessional, and avoid these behaviors during the interview. Also, avoid repeatedly injecting the word "like" or using slang expressions such as "awesome" or "yeah." Do not chew gum.

Use Effective Interpersonal Skills

Focus on using effective verbal and nonverbal interpersonal communication skills. Express yourself with clarity and precision. Use good listening skills, and remain tactful and respectful. Be mindful about excessive hand gesturing as you speak.

Interview Phases

Phase One: Establishing Rapport

A typical interview tends to take place in three phases. In the first phase, you and the interviewer establish rapport by discussing generic topics of possible mutual interest. Be an active listener and focus on the questions initiated by the interviewer. It is helpful to have an idea about the background of your interviewers. The name and title of your interviewers are often provided as part of the interview itinerary and, hopefully, provided in advance. If adequate information about individual interviewers is not provided, you can conduct your own research using the internet or use additional resources such as LinkedIn or the Charlie app at https://charlieapp.com/.

Phase Two: Asking Questions

The next phase involves the detailed part of the interview. It focuses on typical questions related to your qualifications and the position you seek. Listen carefully to the questions and do not hesitate to seek clarification. Answer questions honestly. Often, an interview session becomes a dialogue rather than the interviewer asking questions from a prepared list. A skilled interviewer will direct the discussion through focused questions but will not dominate. Avoid rambling by keeping your comments to less than two minutes per response. You can always take a moment to think about your answer to a specific question, and doing so avoids the appearance of giving a rehearsed response.

Watch for nonverbal cues from the interviewer, such as a raised eyebrow or a loud sigh. If you suspect that the interviewer is not following you, ask, "Would you like me to clarify that?"

Phase Three: Summing It Up

In the final phase, the interviewer may recap key points and make statements such as "We've enjoyed having you here today" to signal that the interview is winding down. At this point, a good interviewer will ask if you have additional questions. This query gives you the opportunity to seek more information and clarify any necessary points. You can also inquire about the timeline for completing the search process and when you may expect any follow-up.

Tip: Give a firm handshake—not too tight or too limp. Pump the interviewer's hand twice and let go.

Cell Phone Etiquette

Many people forget to turn off their cell phones during an interview. And worse, when the phone rings, some people answer the call. Remember that interviewers will evaluate you during every stage of the interview process. Do not interrupt your interview to take calls from others. Play it safe by turning off your cell phone before you enter the office or building of the interview. Do not turn it on again until you are back on the street.

Tip: Do not tell interviewers what you cannot do. Keep a positive attitude. Even if they ask you point blank, never say that you cannot do something. Do not lie, of course. Simply elaborate on an experience that relates to the skill, or say that you are willing to learn.

Topics to Avoid During the Interview

Failure to conform to certain interviewing norms will draw attention to your lack of savvy. Avoid these "red flags":

- Discussing salary and benefits early in the interview process
- Consistently making references to the superiority of the institutions you are associated with
- Speaking negatively about your current or past employers, faculty, or colleagues
- Displaying a "know-it-all" attitude
- Discussing religion, politics, or other highly controversial topics
- Seeking special treatment because of your connections

If you are interested in the position, end the session by letting the interviewer know that. Say that you enjoyed the meeting and look forward to the next step. As you take your leave, make eye contact, smile, and give the interviewer a firm handshake. Since handshake etiquette is important, consider practicing the technique with colleagues in advance of your interview. An example of the technique can be found at https://www.youtube.com/watch?v=IHUAJA2t_NA.

After the Interview

Assess the Experience

After completing the interview session, conduct a brief assessment. Record your personal observations about the environment, staff morale, advancement opportunities, and so on. Evaluate how well the position matches your expectations. How many of your essential attributes does the position provide? What points do you consider negotiable?

Also, conduct a self-assessment of your interviewing skills, and identify areas for improvement. Do you feel happy with the way you answered specific questions? Did you get all the information you were looking for? Did you establish good rapport?

Send a Thank You Note

Soon after the interview, within one or two days, send a letter to your primary interview contact to express thanks and to note your continued enthusiasm about the position. If your contact has been communicating with you electronically, you can consider sending a brief e-mail note of thanks after the interview, followed by a formal typewritten letter. Handwritten notes can be sent to those who participated in your interview, as well as individuals who were supportive during the interview process. Consider letting other contacts in your network know about your interest in the position, especially if they have any close connections with the institution or organization.

Consider the Offer

After the interview process comes the nerve-wracking part of waiting for an acceptance or a rejection. Employers often make rejections by mail and offers by phone. They will follow up a verbal offer with a written letter that conveys important details.

Criteria to focus on as you consider various job offers include

- How well your knowledge, skills, and abilities match your expectations for the position
- The organization's size, management structure, reputation, opportunities for advancement, and work environment
- Geographic location, including cost of living, housing availability, relocation expenses, and climate
- Lifestyle issues such as work schedule, commute time, and opportunity for social activities
- Compensation (e.g., salary, overtime pay, performance bonus) and benefits (e.g., retirement plan options, medical plan options, dental plan, eye care plan, disability insurance, liability insurance, long-term care insurance, tuition waiver plan, flexible spending account, child care, stock options, vacation, holiday time, sick leave)

If you receive several offers that interest you, conduct a thorough evaluation of personal considerations. To compare offers simultaneously, prepare a chart similar to the one in Table 13.1, which shows an evaluation of three hypothetical positions. Consider weighting areas of importance to determine a final score.

TABLE 13.1 Criteria for Evaluating Position Offers

Directions: Determine the level of importance of each criterion by assigning a weighting factor expressed as a percentage of the total. Use the scale below to assign a rating for each criterion pertaining to each position.

Rating Scale: Unacceptable 1 2 3 4 5 6 7 8 9 10 Ideal

		Position A		Position B		Position C	
Criterion	Weighting Factor (%)	Rating (1-10)	Total Score (weight × rate)	Rating (1-10)	Total Score (weight × rate)	Rating (1-10)	Total Score (weight × rate)
Position (match of knowledge, skills, attitudes)	30%	6	1.8	7	2.1	4	1.2
Organization (size, management structure, reputation, opportunities for advancement, work environment)	30%	8	2.4	9	2.7	8	2.4
Geographic location (cost of living, housing availability, climate)	10%	3	0.3	6	0.6	5	0.5
Life style issues (schedule, commute time, social activities)	15%	5	0.8	4	0.6	7	1.1
Compensation (salary, benefits)	15%	5	0.8	8	1.2	9	1.4
Total	100%		6.1		7.2		6.6

CHAPTER 14

Sample Interview Questions

Your ability to answer questions clearly and thoughtfully represents an important part of any interview. Most interviewers rely on a series of questions to determine your suitability for a specific position. They will probably ask some questions related to the hiring organization and the opportunity you seek. Other generic questions will probe your background, communication skills, and personal style.

This chapter provides common questions that you may encounter during an interview session. During any given session, interviewers can ask only a fraction of these questions—but this list will help you brainstorm suitable responses. Yes, you may be a bit overwhelmed by the sheer number of interview questions in the chapter, but the intent is to help you appreciate the broad range of questions that you might be asked.

Take time to think about these questions. You may think you know your life history by heart, but details fade, and without careful reflection, people do not always recognize their own accomplishments. Do not plan out meticulous answers to each question. Focus on questions most closely related to your qualifications and the type of position you seek. You can jot down thoughts and rehearse answers, but do not memorize your responses.

The sample questions are based on themes; thus, selected questions might be applicable to an interview session for a pharmacy technician, student pharmacist, pharmacist (early, mid, or late career), or pharmacists seeking postgraduate programs including residencies, fellowships, or graduate studies.

In all your responses, be brief—no more than 90 to 120 seconds, or a maximum of roughly 350 words. Use positive words and phrases, even when you are discussing difficult topics such as why you left a previous position. (e.g., "I am seeking more challenges," not "I didn't have enough responsibility" or "My boss was a jerk.") Keep your responses focused and give concrete examples of your successes.

This chapter contains several categories of questions. For each category, consider the special points noted as you contemplate possible answers. If you can answer one or two questions from each of the categories, you may be well prepared for your interview.

Accomplishments

Although your résumé or CV may clearly identify your personal and professional accomplishments, you usually get an opportunity during the interview session to discuss them. Routine questions such as "Tell me about your most satisfying accomplishment in life" or "What do you consider your most important idea or suggestion that your current employer implemented?" allows you to focus on one or more of your important accomplishments. In these situations, stay focused on your professional accomplishments. Try to discuss recent ones, because they are fresher in your mind and you will have a better chance of providing specific details. Always include a brief discussion of your accomplishments when you respond to the question "Tell me about yourself." Possible accomplishment questions include the following:

- What do you consider to be your most important idea or suggestion that your current employer implemented?
- Tell me about an award or recognition certificate you have received.
- Tell me about your most satisfying accomplishment in life.
- Tell me about your most satisfying accomplishment as a pharmacist [student pharmacist, technician].
- Tell me how you supported your present or past employer in reaching a departmental goal.
- Tell me about a quantifiable outcome from one of your efforts at work.

Always include a brief discussion of your accomplishments when you respond to the question "Tell me about yourself."

- Describe a technical skill you developed and perfected during the past year.
- How do you measure your success at work?
- How do you handle success?
- Tell me about a time when you completed an assignment that was well received by your employer.
- Tell me which one of your publications gave you the greatest personal satisfaction and why.
- What do you consider the most significant accomplishment in your professional career?
- What achievement at work has given you the greatest sense of personal accomplishment?
- Tell me about a time when your idea or action reduced an expense for your employer.
- Tell me your three most significant accomplishments at your current place of employment. Why do you think your employer considers them important?
- What academic honors or awards did you receive in college?

Career Development

Interviewers like to compare your goals and objectives with those of their organization or program. A career goal statement listed in your résumé or curriculum vitae, although not usually included, can offer a great opening for the discussion. Keep in mind that short-term goals span one or two years, while long-term goals extend three to five years ahead.

Review the organization's goals in advance to ensure compatibility with yours. Most likely, you will want a position that gives you the chance to acquire new knowledge and skills so you can advance within the profession or assume additional responsibilities. Possible career development questions include the following:

- What career goals have you set for the future? Have these changed since you graduated?
- How has your career progressed in relation to your career plan?
- What would you like to accomplish during the next five years?
- How do your current career goals differ from the career goals you set five years ago?
- Have you ever considered leaving the profession of pharmacy? If so, what career choice would you select?
- Tell me why you think this is the right position for you at this point in your career.
- What career plans do you have beyond this position?
- What other career opportunities would you like to experience?
- Which of the career tracks offered by our company do you find most appealing?
- Have you ever considered taking a position that was not part of your career plan?
- If you could begin your career path again, what changes would you make?
- In climbing a career ladder, how critical is it for you to reach the top rung?
- Why have you considered changing your career path in pharmacy at this point in your life?
- Would you like to have your current supervisor's position?
- How much thought do you give to your future?
- To what extent does this position fit with your overall career plan? Does it present inconsistencies with your plan?
- How do you feel about the progress of your career to date?
- Describe the ideal position based on your long-term career plan.
- What are your short-term (one- to two-year) career goals? How do you plan to achieve them?
- What are your long-term (three- to five-year) career goals? How do you plan to achieve them?
- How do you determine if your career plan is on track?
- Why did you decide to pursue a career in pharmacy?
- How do you see your career changing over the next few years? What are you doing to prepare yourself for these changes?
- I noticed that you have not worked for several years. What have you done to keep up with changes in the profession?
- Tell me about the interruptions in your employment history.
- Who had the greatest influence on your choice of pharmacy as a career path?
- Describe a major career planning goal that you recently established for yourself. How do you plan to achieve this goal?
- What area of pharmacy are you most inclined to be involved with after graduation?

Coping with Change

The health care industry involves constant change, and successful employees learn to adapt. The changes discussed in the interview process often focus on technology, human resources, administrative leadership, or professional services. Prepare yourself to share one or more examples of significant change in your present work setting and how you adjusted. Some examples of these questions include the following:

- How do you handle change at work?
- Describe a time you had to change your leadership [management] style.

- Do you prefer a structured routine in your daily work or frequent change?
- Change has contributed to our department's success during the past few years. Tell me about your ability to deal with change.
- Describe a time when a change at work had a significant impact on your work or responsibilities. How did you adjust?
- Tell me about a time when you were involved in a project or assignment at work that resulted in a significant positive [negative] change.
- How do you deal with individuals who resist change?
- Tell me about a time when change led to downsizing in your organization. How did you deal with the situation?

Communication Skills

Pharmacy professionals need strong written and verbal communication skills. Your résumé, curriculum vitae, and cover letters provide key vehicles for demonstrating your writing skills. Interviewers will assess your speaking ability—how clearly and in what manner you convey information—during the interview session. Possible communication-related questions include the following:

- How do you routinely communicate with your subordinates and/or superiors?
- How would you rate your writing abilities?
- How would you rate your oral presentation skills?
- What process do you follow in preparing a presentation?
- How do you "stay connected" with your colleagues?
- Describe your experience in making oral presentations.
- Tell me about a quality presentation you delivered. What made it successful?
- How would you compare your oral presentation skills to your writing skills?
- Do you prefer to write or speak? Why?
- Tell me about your most difficult writing assignment. What did you learn?
- How would you describe your listening skills?
- What is your greatest challenge in responding to electronic messages?

Dealing with Conflict

Conflict exists in any work setting. Interviewers who want to determine your ability to cope with conflict will probably ask situation-based questions such as "Tell me about a time you had to deal with an irate patient. How did you handle the situation?" Most people, even those with modest work experience, can usually discuss one or more incidents involving conflict. Think about past examples with a positive outcome, and relate a story that demonstrates your ability to deal with conflict. Possible conflict-related questions include the following:

Most people, even those with modest work experience, can usually discuss one or more incidents involving conflict.

- Do you prefer to confront conflict or tactfully avoid it?
- How do you go about confronting your colleagues when problems occur?
- How do you attempt to avoid conflict?
- Do you prefer to address small issues before they become problems, or do you wait to see if they resolve on their own?
- Have you ever lost your temper at work?
- How do you handle conflict?
- How do you deal with your colleagues after a difficult situation has been resolved?
- Tell me about a time when you had to deal with an irate patient [physician, nurse, or student]. How did you handle the situation?
- Tell me about a situation in which you avoided siding with a colleague about a difficult issue.
- Tell me about a time when you needed to work closely with someone you routinely disagree with. How did you deal with the situation?
- Describe a time when you successfully resolved a conflict between two of your colleagues.
- How do you deal with "office politics?"
- Tell me about a situation in which you had a personal commitment that resulted in a conflict with your work schedule. What did you do?
- Describe a time when you did not achieve a successful resolution of a conflict with one of your colleagues.
- Describe a time when you did achieve a successful resolution of conflict with one of your colleagues.

Creativity

Employers like to see evidence that employees can be inventive and think "outside the box." Make sure you can present examples from your past work experiences that demonstrate your ability to think creatively in the work setting.

Make sure you can present examples from your past work experiences that demonstrate your ability to think creatively in the work setting.

Some examples of this type of question or request are presented here:

- Tell me about a time while not at work that you got an idea that helped you become more successful at work.
- If you were a drug, what drug would you be? Why?
- Which three adjectives would you use to describe yourself?
- Convince me that I need to buy the chair you are sitting in.
- What would you do if this was your last week on earth?
- How would you like people to remember you?
- Describe your most innovative work assignment.
- Describe a time when your personal creativity helped solve a problem at work.
- Tell me about a time when you improved something that was already working fine.
- Tell me about your participation in a really creative project.
- What areas of research interest you?
- Describe something creative you did as an employee [student].
- If you were hospitalized, with whom would you like to share your semi-private room?
- Tell me about a time when you overcame an obstacle at work when you had limited resources.

Handling Criticism

Dealing with criticism constructively represents an important element of self-assessment and self-improvement. When an interviewer asks how you handle criticism, describe an incident that demonstrates what you learned from the critical comments of a supervisor or coworker. Possible questions or requests concerning this issue include the following:

- Tell me about a time when you were unfairly criticized. How did you handle the situation?
- What is your approach for dealing with constructive criticism?
- If your supervisor was unfair in his or her criticism of your work performance, what would you do?
- Describe a situation in which your work was justifiably criticized.
- What is the most constructive criticism you have ever received?
- What would you do if I said that I thought your interview skills were less than I expect for an individual with your experience?
- Has one of your professors ever assigned a grade lower than you deserved? If so, what did you do?

When an interviewer asks how you handle criticism, describe an incident that demonstrates what you learned from the critical comments of a supervisor or coworker.

Decision-Making Skills

Decision making figures prominently in professional success. Interviewers may ask about the types of decisions you have a difficult time making and how you make decisions in the absence of adequate data. Relate recent examples that demonstrate your ability to make decisions—especially examples related to situations likely to occur in the position you seek. Common questions about decision-making skills include the following:

- On her way to a three-day business meeting, your supervisor leaves an assignment with incomplete and unclear instructions. You have no luck in reaching her. How would you handle this situation?
- Your supervisor directs you to complete an assignment with incorrect instructions. How would you handle this situation?
- What approach do you use to make important decisions?
- How did you handle the most difficult decision you ever had to make?

Relate recent examples that demonstrate your ability to make decisions—especially examples related to situations likely to occur in the position you seek.

- After you make a decision, do you ever change your mind?
- To what extent does intuition play an important part in your decision-making process?
- Tell me about a time when you made an unpopular decision. How did you handle this situation?
- Describe a situation when you had to make a quick decision without the ability to gather all the facts.
- Have you ever made a decision without the knowledge of a standard operating procedure to assist you?
- Give me some examples of decisions that you routinely make in your current position. How do you go about making these decisions?
- Tell me about a time when you had to defend your decision.
- Which types of decisions do you find easy [difficult] to make? Why?
- Think about an important decision that you made in the past. Would you make the same decision today? Why or why not?
- To what extent do you seek information from others before making a decision?
- How have your decision-making skills improved in the last few years? What factors have contributed to this improvement?

Educational Experience

Although interviewers can learn much about your educational experience from your résumé or curriculum vitae, they will probably want to know more about its depth and breadth and how it relates to the position you seek—especially if you are a recent graduate. Stay focused on your academic strengths, and avoid concentrating on weaker academic performance in a specific course. If they consider grades a critical determinant for employment, interviewers probably will have reviewed your academic transcript in advance. No matter what kind of student you were, discuss ways you have successfully applied your knowledge in the work setting. Possible education-related questions include the following:

- Does your overall grade point average on your college transcript adequately reflect your academic ability?
- How do you think your academic performance will correlate with your work performance?
- Where did you rank in your graduating class in high school [college, pharmacy school]?
- Tell me about your most significant interprofessional learning experience as a student pharmacist and why it was significant to you.
- How did you choose the college or university you attended?
- What subjects did you enjoy most [least] in pharmacy school?
- If you had it to do over again, what changes would you make as a pharmacy [college, high school] student?
- If you were entering a pharmacy degree program again, which courses would you devote more time to fully understand?
- In what courses did you earn low [high] grades? How do you think that will affect your work performance?
- What were a few of your most [least] favorite college courses? Why?
- Which year of college was the most difficult for you? Why?
- On average, how many hours do you estimate that you spent studying per week when you were earning your pharmacy degree?
- Did you work full-time or part-time while earning your pharmacy degree?
- What aspects of your pharmacy [college, high school] education did you enjoy most?
- Tell me more about the factors that led you to select the topic for your thesis.
- What are the major findings of your thesis?
- What process did you follow to select your thesis advisor?
- What was the role of your thesis advisor in guiding the completion of your work?
- What publications have resulted from your graduate work?
- How well do you think academic performance correlates with productivity as an employee?

Issues Related to the Employer or Position

Become as familiar as you can with the position description and the organization so you can adeptly handle questions related to the employer and position. Prepare a list of your ideal job or position preferences, such as location, type of

> If asked to talk about your weaknesses, do not describe every flaw you think you have. Simply identify an area that you improved and explain the positive changes that resulted.

practice setting, level of supervision desired, characteristics of ideal colleagues, and work schedule. Also, reflect on your past performance evaluations and prepare to describe the strengths they identified. If asked to talk about your weaknesses, do not spill out every flaw you think you have. Simply identify an area that you improved and explain the positive changes that resulted. Position-related questions or requests for information may include the following:

- What work conditions allow you to perform most successfully in activities you undertake?
- Describe your ideal work environment.
- What do you find most [least] appealing about this position? Why?
- What are your thoughts about customer service?
- What did you learn about us from our website?
- Tell me about a current responsibility that you enjoy as an employee.
- Thinking about your past supervisors, who did you like the most? What were the traits that you liked about this individual?
- Thinking about your past supervisors, who did you like the least? Why? What, if anything, could you have done to improve the relationship?
- If you could change one thing about your most recent employer, what would you change?
- How would your most recent supervisor describe your work habits?
- What do you perceive as differences between this position and your most recent position?
- Tell me about your relationship with your previous supervisors.
- Do you perceive your current or most recent employer as being sensitive to employee needs? Do you think this organization will act differently?
- I see that you have held various jobs. Which one did you like most? Why?
- I see that you have held many jobs for short periods of time. How long would you plan to stay here?
- I see that you have stayed with one employer for a long time. Does this reflect a sense of loyalty or a lack of initiative?
- Why do you want to leave your current position?
- What have your past supervisors identified as your strengths [weaknesses]?
- Describe a typical work day in your most recent position.
- Tell me about a situation at work when you exceeded your supervisor's expectations.
- Would you recommend your most recent employer to your friends? Why or why not?
- Have you ever resigned from a position with less than two weeks' notice? If so, what were the circumstances?
- Have any of your past employers ever refused to give you a reference? If so, what were the circumstances?
- Does your current employer know about this interview today?
- Have you ever been terminated? If so, what were the circumstances?
- Have you ever been asked to resign? If so, what were the circumstances?
- What kind of supervisors motivate you to do your best work?
- How would you describe your current supervisor's management style? Which aspects do you like the most [least]? Why?
- What do you like most [least] about your current position?
- What do you want to achieve in your next position?
- How do you feel about the contributions you made to your most recent employer?
- What has been the pattern of your relationships with supervisors or upper management?
- What would you plan to achieve in this position that you did not achieve in your most recent position?
- What limitations exist in your current position?
- In your most recent position, how much time did you spend working by yourself? Working with others? Do you ever work as a member of a team to complete projects or other assignments?
- In your most recent position, how often did you meet with your supervisor? What was the nature of these meetings?
- Tell me about your last three positions (your major responsibilities, description of the work environment, the relationship with your supervisor and coworkers).
- In your current position, how much time during a typical day do you devote to communications (telephone calls, meetings, presentations, correspondence)?
- If you decide to stay with your current employer, what expectations do you have concerning advancement?
- If you like your current employer and position, why do you plan to leave?
- Since you have expressed difficulties with your current supervisor, what have you done to bring these problems to his or her attention?
- What have you learned from past supervisors?
- How would you characterize the workload associated with your most recent position?

- To what extent has your most recent position prepared you to assume additional responsibilities and duties?
- Describe your relationship and dealings with upper management.
- In your most recent position, what changes did you initiate to enhance the efficiency of the organization?
- Tell me about a situation in your most recent position that you never want to experience again.
- Tell me about a time when your most recent supervisor was not pleased with your job performance.
- Have you ever been denied an opportunity for advancement that you felt you deserved? How did you handle the situation?
- What kind of employee rewards do you like?
- Tell me about a time when you may have expected too much from your employer. How did you handle the situation?
- What skills do you think you need most for success in this position?
- If we hire you for this position, what skills would you like to develop?
- What strengths did you bring to your most recent position that contributed to your success?
- What strengths will make you successful in this position?
- Of the various settings you have worked in, which environment caused you to be the most [least] productive?
- What specific knowledge and skills do you need to improve for successful performance in this position? What can you do to overcome these possible deficiencies?
- How would you rate your potential success in this position? Why?
- What responsibilities in your most recent position did you find difficult to fulfill?
- What would you have liked to achieve in your most recent position that was beyond your reach? Why was it beyond your reach?
- What qualifications do you think you need for this position and how can you satisfy them?
- Tell me what you know about our organization. How did you obtain this information? What did you learn about us from our website?
- What particular aspects of this organization appear most interesting to you?
- Give me your impression of our company within the marketplace.
- Where do you think we are the most vulnerable as an industry?
- From your perspective, describe our company's primary competition.
- What would you do if a competitor offered you a position similar to the one discussed here?
- What trends do you see in our industry?
- If you were in my position, what type of experience would you consider important for this position?
- What do you see in common between this position and your most recent position?
- What differences do you see between this position and your most recent position?
- How did you learn about this open position?
- During the past six months, have you arrived late to work? How often, and what were the circumstances?
- What have you heard about our organization that raises concerns in your mind?
- How will you handle the least appealing aspects of this position?
- What aspects of this position can you fulfill confidently?
- What aspects of this position raise concerns about your abilities?
- In three minutes or less, tell me why we should hire you [why you are the best candidate for this position].
- What process did you use to select your references?
- How long will it take for you to contribute to our organization's success?
- After reviewing your résumé, most reasonable managers might conclude that you have too much experience for this position. What do you think?
- After reviewing your résumé, it appears that you lack the requisite qualifications for this position. Why should I hire you?
- What characteristics do you want most in a position?
- A number of applicants are being interviewed for this position. Why should we consider you for the position?
- Did you consider yourself to have a sense of loyalty to any of your past employers? Why or why not?
- Name one particular characteristic or skill that should make you more successful than other candidates for this position.
- Often, employees are either concept oriented or task oriented. How would you describe yourself?
- Do you enjoy routine tasks and duties at work?

Knowledge of Issues Facing the Profession

Keeping up to date on issues facing the profession remains essential—especially matters that may have a key bearing on the position you seek. Interviewers will probably want you to discuss current issues, including controversial ones within the profession. Possible questions in this area include the following:

- What recommendations can you suggest to improve safe medication practices?
- In your opinion, should the profession support a mandatory reporting system for serious or fatal adverse events?
- What does the term "pharmaceutical care" mean to you?
- As a pharmacist, what would you do to bridge the gap concerning health disparities?
- How do you see the role of the pharmacist changing in the next five years?
- What recommendations would you suggest to support public and private insurance payment to pharmacists for patient services that improve clinical and economic outcomes?
- Should pharmacies sell cigarettes?
- In your opinion, do pharmacists need credentialing to participate in disease state management programs?
- How would you try to initiate a collaborative practice agreement with a physician?
- What clinical evidence exists to support the value of pharmacists in providing patient care services?
- What role does direct-to-consumer advertising play in educating patients about prescription medications?
- What major challenges do you think the profession will face over the next 10 years?
- Describe opportunities for initiating medication therapy management services.
- What measures can pharmacists take to reduce the incidence of medication errors?
- What impact will telemedicine technology have on the practice of pharmacy?
- Should the general public have access to data from clinical drug trials?
- Who should bear responsibility for certifying pharmacists to participate in disease state management activities?
- Which cognitive services provided by pharmacists result in a positive cost benefit to patients and payers?
- Why have pharmacists been ranked as one of the most respected health professionals during the past decade?
- How would you advise a patient to choose his or her personal pharmacist?
- What role should pharmacists play in response to a disaster such as an influenza pandemic?
- How can technology enhance the role of the practicing pharmacist?
- Tell me about two major accomplishments of the Joint Commission of Pharmacy Practitioners during the past decade.
- What changes would you like to see in the U.S. health care system?
- How does medication therapy management relate to health care reform?
- What is the future impact of e-prescribing on the pharmacy profession?
- How can pharmacists reduce antibiotic resistance?
- What single greatest challenge does the profession face in the next two years?
- What important trends do you see in our profession?
- What do you feel it takes to be a professional?
- What does the term "professionalism" mean to you?
- What does it mean to be a professional?
- Tell me about a time when you displayed professionalism.
- Describe an ethical dilemma you faced in a practice situation. How did you deal with it?

Leadership Qualities

Although they relate directly to people seeking administrative responsibilities, questions about leadership qualities may apply to any position within the profession. Most interviewers will want to determine your ability to serve as a role model for others. When responding, try to use the term "we" rather than "I" to suggest that you value and make the most of teamwork. Leadership-related questions or requests may include the following:

- What leadership positions, if any, did you hold in pharmacy student organizations? How were you selected for these positions?

Most interviewers will want to determine your ability to serve as a role model for others.

- Tell me about a time when you persuaded others to accept your recommendation or advice.
- How would a coworker describe your leadership style?
- Describe the characteristics of a leader you admire.
- Tell me about a time when you led a project with a positive [negative] outcome.
- What kept you from greater participation in extra-curricular activities when you were in pharmacy school [college, high school]?
- How do you go about influencing someone to accept your ideas?
- Tell me about a memorable leadership experience you had?
- Tell me about your commitment to maintaining a diverse work force.
- Give me examples of how you have demonstrated leadership qualities in your current position.
- Who is your favorite leader in pharmacy? Why?
- Tell me about an effective leader you have known. In your opinion, what made this individual effective?

Commitment to Life-Long Learning

Because knowledge in the health care community expands so rapidly, you must commit yourself to continual learning. Pharmacy school provides a great foundation, but you must take an active role in your learning upon graduation. At interviews, discuss your continuing education programs, professional meetings, certificate programs, or other types of learning programs. Questions interviewers may ask you include the following:

- Describe your three most significant learning experiences during the past six months.
- Do you plan to pursue additional studies?
- How much time do you spend each month keeping up with the professional literature? Which professional journals do you routinely read?
- Do you currently take, or do you plan to take, evening courses?
- Do you subscribe to any professional journals? Which ones?
- In the last year, what type of pharmacy continuing education programs have you attended?
- How do you keep up with the scientific advances in drug therapy?

Management Skills and Abilities

When you apply for a supervisory position, you will be asked questions related to management abilities. These questions probe specific skills such as planning, organizing, directing, and controlling. Review the duties you carried out in your past positions to help you provide specific examples. Possible questions to determine your management skills include the following:

> Management-related questions probe specific skills such as planning, organizing, directing, and controlling.

- Have you overseen budgeting, approved expenses, and monitored departmental progress against financial goals? How qualified do you feel in performing these activities?
- Tell me about your supervision of other individuals in your past positions.
- What is the most important management skill you learned from a single experience?
- Tell me about a learning experience that affected your management style.
- Give me examples of what you did in your most recent position to increase revenues and reduce costs.
- Have you ever had to hire people? For what types of positions?
- What characteristics do you look for in individuals you plan to hire?
- Have you ever fired anyone? What were the circumstances?
- What type of management style do you think proves effective in managing health professionals?
- Describe your management style. What aspects would you like to change? Why?
- Tell me about a time when you did not receive full support in the completion of a task and how you dealt with it.
- Are you an effective manager? Give me examples of your management effectiveness.
- Tell me about the people you hired in your current job. How long did they stay with you? How did their coworkers view them?
- What process would you use to address an employee with an unsatisfactory performance evaluation?
- How do you identify deficiencies in your subordinates?
- Give examples of your ability to delegate.
- Tell me about a time when you dealt with an employee displaying inappropriate behavior in your work setting.

- What characteristics does an effective department director display?
- How would you describe your management philosophy?
- Give me examples of how you balance autonomy and control among your employees.
- How do you effectively evaluate the performance of your staff?
- How would your staff describe your management style?
- What techniques have you found effective for motivating your staff?
- Tell me about one of your former employees who was promoted as a result of your mentoring.
- How do you prefer to recognize and reward your staff for excellent work performance?
- How do you train and develop your staff?
- How do you differentiate between management and leadership?
- Would you describe yourself as a manager or a leader? Can you elaborate?
- Give me examples of your ability to manage resources effectively.
- Tell me about a time when you negotiated a conflict between two of your most [least] successful employees.
- What strengths [weaknesses] do you display as a manager?
- If you left your current position, do you have someone to take your place? How have you developed this person to assume your responsibilities?
- Give examples of how you enhanced the effectiveness of your immediate superior in your most recent position.
- Tell me about your experience in dealing with external consultants. How did you use their recommendations for improving your department?
- Tell me about a time when you made a bad hiring decision.
- What process have you found useful in planning?
- How do you go about organizing and planning for the successful completion of a major project or event?
- Give me examples of how you handle multiple projects or assignments.
- Tell me about a time when you became sidetracked with the details of an assignment.
- How would you describe your attitude toward taking risks?
- How do you respond to the concept of "no risk, no reward?"
- What risks did you take in your most recent position? What results did taking these risks achieve?
- Do you consider yourself a risk taker? Give me examples of risks you have taken in previous positions.
- Tell me about an experience at work where the risks outweighed the rewards. How did you deal with this situation?
- How did you go about obtaining your most recent position?

Maintaining Peer Relationships

Pharmacy professionals must work as a team, not only within the profession but with members of the other health disciplines. Employers and program directors want to know that you have effective interpersonal skills for building and maintaining positive relationships. Interviewers will observe how well you relate to others and want to hear current examples of your skills, especially how you deal with "difficult" personality styles. Possible questions about your peer relationships include the following:

- Describe your working relationship with peers.
- When assigned to a team, what are the qualities you like most in a team member?
- How would you describe your coworkers at your most recent place of employment?
- How do you deal with weaknesses in others?
- What do you consider the ideal mix of individuals for a productive work team?
- How would you compare the quality and quantity of your work to that of your coworkers?
- Do you prefer working alone or with others?
- In your most recent position, how did you relate to coworkers with more [fewer] years of experience?
- How do you like to work with other people when completing projects?
- Tell me about your ability to get along with classmates [faculty members, coworkers].
- What types of people irritate you at work?

> Interviewers will observe how well you relate to others and want to hear current examples of your skills.

- Tell me about the types of people you like to associate with at work.
- Do you enjoy meeting people?
- Tell me about a time when you were not successful in getting along with a coworker. How did you resolve the issue?

Personal Attributes

Most of us do not normally recite a litany of our personal strengths, but in an interview you must do just that. Emphasize attributes such as exhibiting a strong work ethic and being self-motivated, enthusiastic, loyal, a team player, dependable, flexible, and caring. When discussing attributes, tie their relevance to the position you seek. Possible personal attribute questions include the following:

- What personal characteristics do you consider ideal for a pharmacist? How do these match your personal characteristics? How do they differ?
- What makes you different from other pharmacists [technicians, students, employees]?
- How do you measure personal success?
- Give me examples of your determination.
- Describe a time when you spoke up for others.
- Who is your mentor? Why?
- Tell me about a time when your persistence paid off at work.
- How do I know you are a sincere person?
- How hard have you worked to achieve your career goals?
- Tell me about a time when you were right, but others disagreed. How did you deal with the situation?
- Tell me about a time when you accomplished a task that required a significant amount of discipline.
- In your most recent position, did you work harder than your coworkers?
- What motivates you to excel?
- List five things that motivate you to do your best work.

Emphasize attributes such as exhibiting a strong work ethic and being self-motivated, enthusiastic, loyal, a team player, dependable, flexible, and caring.

- Are you self-motivated? Give me examples of how you display initiative at work.
- How do you motivate other people?
- How has competition affected your achievements? Give me examples of positive [negative] impacts.
- What personal rewards do you want from your job?
- Tell me about a long-standing interest or activity of yours.
- How do you unwind in your spare time?
- What percent of your college expenses did you earn? How?
- What did you do during your summers while you were in college?
- How do you balance your outside activities with your work?
- Tell me about a movie that inspired you.
- Do you enjoy reading? What is your favorite book [magazine]?
- Tell me about the last book you read.
- How would your best friend [college roommate, favorite supervisor, coworkers] describe you?
- If you could change one thing about your personality, what would it be? Why?
- How do you like to spend your time relaxing when not at work?
- Tell me about a time when you demonstrated a caring attitude.
- What section of the daily newspaper do you like most?
- What television program do you like most?
- Do you include coworkers in your social life?
- Tell me about an interesting trip you have taken.
- How would you describe your personality?
- What importance do you place on being liked by your colleagues?
- Who do you consider your best friend? Why is this individual special to you?
- Tell me something about yourself that you have not included in your résumé.
- Will you relocate, if necessary?
- What will you do if we do not offer this position to you?
- How do you feel about having a dress code in a work environment made up of health professionals?
- Tell me about yourself.
- If I could remember only one thing about you, what should it be?
- How do you feel about being tested for drug use?
- How do you explain your career success?

Interviewers will want to measure your ability to think problems through, apply knowledge, and develop effective solutions.

Problem-Solving Skills

Pharmacy professionals face many problems on a daily basis. Interviewers will want to determine your ability to think problems through, apply knowledge, and develop effective solutions. Questions about problem-solving skills may include the following:

- Tell me about a recurring work problem that you resolved.
- Give me examples of major projects you have completed.
- Tell me about a time when you were assigned to complete an unpopular task. What was the outcome?
- How do you usually approach solving problems?
- Where do you turn when your usual problem-solving approaches do not work?
- Give me examples of how you have used problem-solving techniques successfully.
- Tell me about the most difficult problem you ever confronted.
- Give me an example of a problem that was not resolved to your satisfaction.
- How do you approach problems or difficult assignments that you would prefer to avoid?
- Describe a situation where you were not successful in resolving a problem. How did you finally deal with this situation?
- Tell me about a time when you were asked to solve a problem without sufficient resources. How did you resolve the problem?
- If you encounter an unsatisfied patient, what do you typically do?
- Tell me about a time when you used a creative approach to solve a difficult problem.
- Tell me about a time when you overlooked a simple solution to solve a problem.

Professional and Other Employment Experience

Experiential learning allows you to apply a wide range of knowledge and skills. In describing your past positions, highlight the skills you developed and the aspects of your work that you liked. You also can touch on the aspects you disliked—without going overboard or sounding too negative. It helps to prepare a list of the characteristics you associate with the ideal work setting. Questions about professional experience may include the following:

- What do you consider the most important thing you have learned from your most recent position?
- How will your military experience assist you with the responsibilities of this position?
- As a recent graduate, how will you compensate for your lack of experience in this position?
- Tell me about a time when you were glad that you were the technician/intern and not the pharmacist.
- Do you believe your qualifications [professional experiences] will help you to become successful in this position?
- How does your current position relate to the mission and goals of the organization?
- How do you rate your clinical knowledge and skills?
- How do you rate your past experience in relation to the responsibilities of this position?
- I see that you have held a variety of positions. Overall, what have you learned from your work experience?
- Which of your experiential education experiences was the most [least] professionally satisfying? Why?
- What would your pharmacist preceptors tell me about your ability to apply knowledge in a practice setting?
- Tell me about your experience in preparing and compounding intravenous admixture preparations.
- Give me examples of recommendations you have made to physicians about medication treatment plans that reduced the risk of patient harm.
- Tell me about the outcome of a clinical intervention that you made within the past two months.
- Tell me about your experience in promoting rational drug therapy based on the use of a formulary.
- What approach do you use to document the impact of your patient interventions?
- Give me examples of your interactions with other health care providers in caring for patients.
- During the last year, have you participated in any health care promotion activities? What were the impacts?
- Give me examples of your participation in the activities of local, state, or national pharmacy organizations.
- What makes you an effective teacher?
- Tell me about your experiences in precepting student pharmacists in the practice setting.

If salary-related questions come up in the interview, you can answer them in a positive way without stating your actual salary expectations.

- Your résumé indicates that you have been working as a part-time pharmacy technician. How will this experience help you achieve your career goals?

Salary Issues

Ideally, you will not have to talk about salary until you receive a job offer. If salary-related questions come up in the interview, you can answer them in a positive way without stating your actual salary expectations. For example, you might say that you have an idea of the market, but for the moment you would like to hear more about the position. Or you might say that you find it difficult to formulate salary expectations without knowing the complete benefits package and the nature of the work environment. If you filled out an application form, you may have provided your current salary, so make sure you quote the same amount to the interviewer, if asked. When discussing salary, remember to focus on the total compensation package and not merely the pay. Possible salary-related questions include the following:

- What would you like to earn five years from now?
- Do you believe your current salary reflects your experience and performance evaluations?
- How do you feel about a reduction in salary from your most recent position?
- How much do you value job security?
- Tell me about your salary expectations.
- Have you ever been denied a salary increase? What were the circumstances?
- What do you currently earn?
- What do you expect for a compensation package?

Dealing with Self-Assessment

Everyone has strengths and weaknesses, but when asked "self-assessment" questions, people commonly focus more on the areas in which they need improvement. When discussing deficiencies, emphasize your awareness of the problems and your actions for improvement. Similarly, identify one or two strengths and describe how they positively impact the position you seek. Self-assessment questions may include the following:

When discussing deficiencies, emphasize your awareness of the problem and your actions for improvement. Similarly, identify one or two strengths and describe how they positively impact the position you seek.

- If you could change one thing about yourself, what would you change? Why?
- What adjectives would you use to describe yourself?
- What do you consider your biggest strengths [weaknesses]?
- How does your personality manifest itself when you deal with stressful situations at work?
- Tell me about a time when you failed. How did you handle the situation?
- Do you consider yourself successful? Why?
- To what degree were you satisfied with your performance in your most recent position?
- How would you describe yourself when you were in college? How have you changed since graduating?
- What experience do you need most to advance your career?
- What do you consider the greatest disappointment in your career, to date? How did you overcome it?
- How would you characterize the quality and quantity of your work in your past positions?
- What have you learned from your mistakes?
- Describe a life-changing moment for you.
- What was the most difficult life lesson that you have had to learn?
- How do you reconcile any differences between reality and your expectations?
- What tasks or duties do you find difficult? What have you done to overcome these difficulties?
- How would you rank yourself among your peers based on your work ethic?
- Tell me about a time at work when you were disappointed with your performance.
- Have you ever been called on by one of your professors when you were unsure about the answer? How did you respond?
- What do you consider the most intellectually challenging activity you have ever performed?

- How important do you consider details?
- What plan do you have for improving your professional qualifications?
- Have you considered pursuing an advanced degree?
- What plan do you have for improving your knowledge and skills?
- What work habits have you sought to improve?
- During the past three years, what have you done to improve your professional knowledge and skills?

Stress Management

If managed properly, stress can positively impact a situation. Make sure you can discuss your approaches for coping with stress. Also, provide examples of working under pressure, especially those with positive outcomes. Possible questions about managing stress include the following:

- How do you respond to deadlines?
- Tell me about your ability to work under pressure.
- How do you manage stress in your daily work?
- How do you handle stressful situations with your supervisor [coworkers]?
- Tell me about a time when you worked under significant pressure to meet a deadline.
- What measures do you take to avoid burnout?

Teamwork

People rarely work in isolation. Teamwork applies in just about every work environment, especially in pharmacy practice settings. Recall one or more experiences you had as a team member at work and describe your contribution to the team. Possible questions concerning teamwork may include the following:

- How do you feel as a team member when your project is not successful? How do you deal with the situation?
- How do you promote "esprit de corps" among members of a team at work?
- Do you consider yourself a team player?
- Describe a situation when the team fell apart. What was your role in the outcome?
- Tell me about a time when you were effective in convincing team members to adopt your recommendation.
- Tell me about a contribution you made as a member of a team at work.
- What qualities make you a successful team member?
- Tell me about a time when you had to deal with another team member who was not pulling their weight.
- Tell me about a time when you increased your productivity by serving as a team member at work.
- What type of role do you generally assume when assigned to a team?
- Tell me about a time when you learned about teamwork through your participation in a sport.
- What quality do you value the most in a team member?

Technical Knowledge and Skills

Some employers may want to examine your technical knowledge, assess your skills at applying it, and gauge your ability to "think on your feet." To do this, they might have you review a scenario commonly associated with the position you seek. For example, they might ask a pharmacist seeking a clinical specialist position to review a patient case and develop an optimal drug treatment plan. Questions that employers may ask include the following:

- Describe your familiarity with computer systems and software applications.
- What is the latest computer software application that you have learned?
- Review the following case of a patient with [a common chronic or acute disease], and outline a plan for drug therapy management.
- Review the following case of a patient with [a common, chronic or acute disease] and [any other common, chronic or acute disease]. Outline a plan for drug therapy management.
- Review the following case that describes a common drug interaction [adverse drug reaction]. How would you resolve the problem?
- Review the following case that describes a patient with a history of medication noncompliance. Design a plan to improve the patient's behavior in taking medications.
- Review the following case of a patient with diabetes [seizure disorder, high blood pressure, lipid disorder, congestive heart failure, tuberculosis, bipolar disease,

> Some employers may want to examine your technical knowledge, assess your skills at applying it, and gauge your ability to "think on your feet."

urinary tract infection, Parkinson's disease]. Outline a plan for drug therapy management.
- Review the following case of a patient with bronchitis and a history of anxiety. Outline a plan for drug therapy management.
- Review the following case of a patient with asthma and contact dermatitis. Outline a plan for drug therapy management.
- Review the following case of a patient with rheumatoid arthritis and a duodenal ulcer. Outline a plan for drug therapy management.
- Review the following case of a patient with angina pectoris and deep vein thrombosis. Outline a plan for drug therapy management.
- Review the following case of a patient with bacterial pneumonia and congestive heart failure. Outline a plan for drug therapy management.
- Review the following case of a patient with atrial fibrillation and a history of migraine headaches. Outline a plan for drug therapy management.
- Review the following case of a patient with chronic depression and symptoms of the common cold. Outline a plan for drug therapy management.

Time Management Skills

Success in almost any position requires the ability to set goals, prioritize tasks, and manage time. Interviewers will want to hear specific examples of how you manage your time and what tools you find useful, such as a daily calendar or personal data assistants. Make sure you can answer the following questions:

- Tell me about a time when you did not meet an important deadline. What steps have you taken to avoid this situation in the future?
- How much time did you devote to outside work while you were completing your pharmacy [college, high school] degree?
- What approach do you use for time management?
- Give me examples of how you prioritized work assignments in your most recent position. How do you schedule them so that you can meet deadlines?
- Tell me about a time you requested an extension to complete an important assignment.
- Tell me about a time when you completed an important assignment ahead of schedule.
- Describe your typical workday [work week].
- How do you organize your daily assignments and activities?
- Give me an example of a time management skill that has increased your productivity at work.
- Tell me how you deal with procrastination.

Volunteerism

Your work as a volunteer provides evidence of your ability to share time and expertise with others. The skills you develop doing volunteer activities also can prove to be as valuable as those acquired through paid work. Prepare a list of your volunteer efforts, including professional organizations and community service projects, and think about how each experience has enhanced your career. In what ways might the things you learned as a volunteer contribute to the position you seek? Questions that you may need to answer include the following:

- Tell me about your association with community service organizations. To what extent have you been involved?
- Have you held any positions in a community service organization? If so, to what extent were you involved? What did you gain from the experience?
- Have you ever been considered for a public office? What were the circumstances? What did you gain from the experience?
- Tell me about your involvement in extracurricular activities as a student pharmacist.
- What organizations did you belong to as a student pharmacist?
- Which organizations did you enjoy the most [least]?
- Our organization believes that employees should give time back to the community. How do you feel about this?
- What professional-based community projects interest you?
- Would you consider volunteering as a member of our organization if we did not hire you as an employee?

Issues Related to Mid-Career Interviewees

The pharmacy profession has undergone many changes in the last several decades. Mid-career pharmacists seeking employment today are often competing with recent graduates who have received a different education and experiential experience. To avoid intimidation and discouragement, present yourself as an experienced pharmacist who has a dedicated work ethic and who is mature, a life-long learner, and an effective communicator who is not afraid of technology and the myriad of changes that have occurred in the profession since your graduation. Although some questions might border on age discrimination, a positive attitude combined with experience and maturity can help to overcome the potential bias of an employer. In addition to any of the other questions in this chapter, questions for mid-career interviewees may include the following:

- Tell me about your approach to completing your continuing education requirements during the past three years.
- When were you most satisfied as a pharmacist?
- What motivated you to apply for this position?
- What can you do for us that a new practitioner could not?
- Are you overqualified for this position?
- Tell me about your experience in working with millennials.
- How do you explain your gap in employment?
- This is a fast-paced setting. Will you be able to keep up?
- Tell me about your experience in adapting to changes in technology.
- How do you explain the many different employers you have had in the past ten years?
- How do you feel about reporting to a younger pharmacist?
- Tell me about your experiences as a volunteer.
- Tell me about how you dealt with a significant change you encountered in the past three years.
- Tell me about a time when you served as a mentor to a student pharmacist or colleague.
- Tell me about your experience in dealing with other health professionals.

Concluding the Interview

Questions that interviewers use to wrap up the session can serve as effective segues into your own questions. Always prepare at least three to five questions to ask if the opportunity comes up. In addition, have at least one suitable response in mind if the interviewer asks "Is there anything else I should know about you?" or "Is there anything else I should ask?" Possible questions for concluding the interview include the following:

- In what respect does our position and your needs appear to be a good match? In what respect do they differ?
- Tell me the first three things you would do if you were hired tomorrow.
- Is there anything else I should ask?
- Is there anything else you would like to tell us about yourself?
- Is there anything that will keep you from taking this position if we offer it?
- When can you start work?
- Now that we have spent some time orienting you to the position, what level of interest do you have?
- How does this position compare with other positions you are considering?

Discriminatory Questions

Federal laws do not permit discriminatory questions about your race, color, religion, sex, national origin, marital status, age, or disability.* Although experienced interviewers do not usually ask illegal questions, inexperienced or improperly prepared interviewers might. You may choose to answer an illegal question if you think you can get by with an indirect response. For example, if asked about your plans for marriage, you could say that you do not intend for your personal life to interfere with your work performance. Or you could ask the interviewer to explain how this information relates to the position and then give a similar response. Depending on the circumstances, a direct response such as "I would rather not answer that question" may suffice. Federal laws consider the following sample questions illegal:

- How old are you?
- What is your birth date?
- Are you a citizen of the United States?
- When did you become a citizen of the United States?
- Where were your parents born?
- What is your native language?
- What is your maiden name?
- Our staff is young. How do you think you will fit in?
- What is your religion?
- Does your religion keep you from working on weekends or holidays?
- Do you feel that your race will help you be more effective in this position?
- Who do you live with?
- What is your marital status?
- Where does your spouse work?
- What are your plans for starting a family?
- Other than traffic violations, have you ever committed an unlawful act?
- How many children do you have?
- You mentioned that you have two children. Would this keep you from overnight travel assignments?
- Can you make child care arrangements?
- What is your sexual preference?
- Have you ever been arrested?
- Would you prefer to be addressed as Miss or Mrs.?
- Did you receive an honorable discharge from the military service?
- How tall are you?
- How much do you weigh?
- Have you ever filed for bankruptcy?
- Do you have a good credit rating?
- Do you have any disabilities?
- What can you tell me about your medical history?
- Have you ever received workers' compensation?
- Have you ever been treated for alcoholism or drug dependence?
- Have you ever been hospitalized?
- Do you have any health conditions that would compromise your attendance record?
- How many days of work did you miss last year because of illness?
- Are you concerned that you do not have an advanced degree?
- Have you had any recent or past illnesses or operations?
- Do you belong to any social, religious, or community groups?

* The relevant federal laws include Title VII of the Civil Rights Act of 1964; Age Discrimination in Employment Act of 1967; Title I of the Americans with Disabilities Act of 1990; The Rehabilitation Act of 1973; The Vietnam Era Veteran's Readjustment Act of 1974; Executive Order 11246.

Questioning the Interviewer

Interviewers expect intelligent questions from successful candidates. The chance to ask questions generally occurs throughout the interview process, especially if the process is informal. Even in a formal interview process, an opportunity will arise when the interviewer invites questions. Make sure you ask questions relevant to the position. Before the interview, prepare a written list of questions for which you would like answers. You may choose to glance at the list during your interview session if you cannot remember specific questions. Two or three questions should suffice, because you can always follow up with additional questions if you receive an offer. You may also ask the interviewer if he or she minds if you take notes. The following list contains examples of questions you can ask:

- If I succeed in this position, what opportunities will I have to advance within the organization?
- Do you feel that I have the qualifications needed for success in this position?
- Where do you see the organization during the next three to five years?
- What relationship exists between this department and senior management?
- What attracted you to this organization?
- What do you like about working here?
- What organizational changes do you expect within the next year?
- How do other departments in the organization view this department?
- How receptive are other health professionals in your organization to clinical intervention recommendations made by pharmacists?
- Do you encourage participation in community service and professional organizations?
- What do you consider the primary reason for your organization's success?
- How does management respond to staff ideas?
- What immediate challenges face your department?
- What are the most significant challenges the person in this position will face?
- What types of pharmacists [employees] generally succeed in your organization?
- What pharmacists will I work with? Will I be able to meet them?
- How would you describe your management style?
- What personal qualities do you like most in your employees?
- What would a successful first year in this position look like?
- What changes would you expect the next person who fills this position to make?
- Does your staff ever socialize outside work?
- To what extent do senior managers solicit ideas and invite feedback from staff members?
- Why is this position available?
- Can you describe a typical work week for someone in this position?
- What type of orientation will I receive if I am hired?
- Would I be responsible for supervising other staff? If so, how many and what type of positions?
- What kinds of assignments should I anticipate during the first six months in the position?
- What aspect of this position do you consider most difficult?
- What did you like most about the person who previously held this position?
- What are your immediate priorities for the person who fills this position?
- How would you describe the ideal candidate for this position?
- When you think about employees who have succeeded in this position, what kind of qualities did they usually have?
- Do you have any concerns about my experience or skills?
- What opportunities exist for continuing my education?
- Have you experienced any staff reductions in the past three years?
- What is the turnover rate among pharmacists in your organization?
- Do you encourage employees to become active in professional associations?
- What types of training and development do you provide for the advancement of an individual in this position?
- Do you have a tuition reimbursement program? If so, how does it work?
- Do you have a management development program?
- What do your employees like most [least] about working here?
- What does a typical weekly schedule look like for this position?
- What are two or three of the most important criteria that you will use to select the candidate for this position?
- What are the most difficult adjustments that new employees face when joining your department?
- How would you describe the department's culture?
- Are there any reservations you have about my qualifications for the position that I can attempt to address?
- What is your time frame for getting back with candidates about a hiring decision?
- Is there anything else I can provide to help you with your decision about me?

Supplementary Information Sources

APPENDIX

A wealth of reference materials exist about career planning, interviewing skills, and preparing correspondence. Although most of these publications have been prepared with the business community in mind, the principles apply to other professionals, as well. The sources in the following reference list may provide useful information.

Career Planning

American Pharmacists Association (APhA) Career Pathway Evaluation Program for Pharmacy Professionals, 2012 Pharmacist Profile Survey. Washington, DC: American Pharmacists Association; 2012.

Andrusia D, Haskins R. *Brand Yourself.* New York: Ballantine Publishing Group; 2000.

APhA Career Pathway Evaluation Program for Pharmacy Professionals. 6th ed. Washington, DC: American Pharmacists Association; 2007.

Askew JP. *From Student to Pharmacist.* Washington, DC: American Pharmacists Association; 2010.

Baker WE. *Networking Smart.* Lincoln, NE: Backinprint.com; 2000.

Boddy S. *Powerful Unemployment.* North Charleston, SC: BookSurge; 2009.

Bolles ME, Bolles RN. *Job-Hunting Online.* 6th ed. Berkeley: Ten Speed Press; 2011.

Bolles RN. *What Color Is Your Parachute? 2017: A Practical Manual for Job-Hunters and Career-Changers.* Berkeley: Ten Speed Press; 2016.

Gurney DW. *Headhunters Revealed!* Los Angeles: Hunter Arts Publishing; 2000.

Holdford DA. Managing yourself: an essential skill for managing others. *J Am Pharm Assoc.* 2009;49(3):436–445.

Levinson JC, Perry DE. *Guerrilla Marketing for Job Hunters 3.0.* Hoboken, NJ: John Wiley and Sons; 2011.

Miller, ML. *Getting Started in a Pharmacy Residency.* Washington, DC: American Pharmacists Association; 2013.

Myers FR. *Get the Job You Want Even When No One's Hiring.* Hoboken, NJ: John Wiley and Sons; 2009.

Pierson O. *The Unwritten Rules of the Highly Effective Job Search.* New York: McGraw-Hill Companies; 2006.

Rath T. *Strengths Finder 2.0.* New York: Gallup Press; 2007.

Schommer JC, Brown LM, Sogol EM. Identifying work setting profile factors from the Career Pathway Evaluation Program. *Am J Pharm Educ.* 2013;77(9):194.

Schommer JC, Brown LM, Sogol EM. *APhA Career Pathway Evaluation Program 2007 Pharmacist Profile Survey.* Washington, DC: American Pharmacists Association; June 2007.

Schommer JC, Sogel EM, Brown LM. Career pathways for pharmacists. *J Am Pharm Assoc.* 2007;47(5):14–15.

Schommer JC, Brown LM, Millonig MK, Sogol EM. Career Pathways Evaluation Program: 2002 Pharmacist Profile Survey. *Am J Pharm Educ.* 2003;67:Article 79.

Vick JM, Furlong JS. *The Academic Job Search Handbook.* 5th ed. Philadelphia: University of Pennsylvania Press; 2016.

Preparing Résumés and Curricula Vitae

Asher D. *The Overnight Résumé.* 3rd ed. Berkeley: Ten Speed Press; 2010.

Block JA, Betrus M. *202 Great Résumés.* Washington, DC: McGraw-Hill Companies; 2004.

Block JA, Betrus M. *101 Best Résumés to Sell Yourself.* Washington, DC: McGraw-Hill Companies; 2002.

Corwin G, Grappo GJ, Lewis A. *How to Write Better Résumés.* 6th ed. New York: McGraw-Hill Companies; 2003.

Criscito P. *e-Résumés: A Guide to Successful Online Job Hunting.* 4th ed. Hauppauge, NY: Barron's Educational Series; 2005.

Criscito P. *Designing the Perfect Résumé.* 3rd ed. Hauppauge, NY: Barron's Educational Series; 2000.

Enelow WS, Kursmark LM. *Expert Résumés for People Returning to Work.* 2nd ed. Indianapolis, IN: JIST Works; 2007.

Enelow WS, Kursmark LM. *Expert Résumés for Career Changers.* 2nd ed. Indianapolis, IN: JIST Works; 2010.

Enelow WS. *Best Key Words for Résumés, Cover Letters and Interviews: Powerful Communications Tools for Success.* Manassas Park, VA: Impact Publications; 2003.

Farr JM. *The Quick Résumé and Cover Letter Book.* 5th ed. Indianapolis, IN: JIST Works; 2011.

Greene B. *Get the Interview Every Time.* Chicago: Dearborn Trade Publishing; 2008.

Ireland S. *The Complete Idiot's Guide to the Perfect Résumé.* 5th ed. New York: Penguin Putnam; 2010.

Isaacs K, Hofferber K. *The Career Change Résumé.* New York: McGraw-Hill Companies; 2003.

Jackson AL, Geckeis K. *How to Prepare Your Curriculum Vitae.* 3rd ed. New York: McGraw-Hill Companies; 2003.

Kennedy JL. *Résumés for Dummies.* 6th ed. Foster City, CA: IDG Books Worldwide; 2011.

Krannich RL, Enelow WS. *Best Résumés and CVs for International Jobs.* Manassas Park, VA: Impact Publications; 2002.

Krannich RL, Banis WJ. *High Impact Résumés and Letters.* 9th ed. Manassas Park, VA: Impact Publications; 2006.

Marino K. *Résumés for the Health Care Professional.* New York: John Wiley and Sons; 2000.

Nadler BJ. *The Everything Résumé Book.* 3rd ed. Avon, MA: Adams Media; 2008.

Noble DF. *Gallery of Best Résumés.* 5th ed. Indianapolis, IN: JIST Works Inc; 2012.

Provenzano SA. *Top Secret Executive Résumés.* 2nd ed. Boston: Course Technology; 2011.

Ryan R. *Winning Résumés.* 2nd ed. New York: John Wiley and Sons; 2002.

Troutman KK. *The Federal Résumé Guidebook: Write a Winning Federal Résumé to Get in, Get Promoted, and Survive in a Government Career!* 3rd ed. Indianapolis, IN: JIST Works; 2004.

Troutman KK. *Federal Résumé Guidebook.* 4th ed. Indianapolis, IN: JIST Works; 2007.

Tysinger JW. *Résumés and Personal Statements for Health Professionals.* 2nd ed. Tucson: Galen Press, Ltd; 1999.

VGM Career Horizons. *Résumés for Health and Medical Careers.* 4thed. New York: McGraw-Hill; 2008.

Whitcomb SB. *Résumé Magic: Trade Secrets of a Professional Résumé Writer.* 4th ed. Indianapolis, IN: JIST Works; 2010.

Wilson RF, Lewis A. *Better Résumés for Executives and Professionals.* 4th ed. Hauppauge, NY: Barron's Educational Series; 2000.

Interviewing Skills

Allen JG. *The Complete Q & A Job Interview Book.* 4th ed. New York: John Wiley and Sons; 2004.

Beatty RH. *The Interview Kit.* 3rd ed. New York: John Wiley and Sons; 2003.

Camp R, Vielhaber ME, Simonetti JL. *Strategic Interviewing.* San Francisco: Jossey-Bass; 2001.

DeLuca MJ. DeLuca NF. *More Best Answers to the 201 Most Frequently Asked Interview Questions.* 2nd ed. Washington, DC: McGraw-Hill Companies; 2010.

Drake J. *The Perfect Interview: How to Get the Job You Really Want.* 2nd ed. New York: AMACOM; 2011.

Fein R. *101 Dynamite Questions to Ask at Your Job Interview.* 2nd ed. Manassas Park, VA: Impact Publications; 2000.

Fry R. *101 Great Answers to the Toughest Interview Questions.* Wayne, NJ: Career Press; 2016.

Kador J. *301 Best Questions to Ask on Your Interview.* 2nd ed. New York: McGraw-Hill Companies; 2010.

Kennedy JL. *Job Interviews for Dummies.* 4th ed. New York: IDG Books Worldwide; 2011.

Krannich CR, Krannich RL. *Interview for Success.* 8th ed. Manassas Park, VA: Impact Publications; 2002.

McKay DR. *The Everything Practice Interview Book.* 2nd ed.Avon, MA: Adams Media; 2009.

Martin C. *Boost Your Interview IQ.* 2nd ed. New York: McGraw-Hill; 2012.

Medley HA. *Sweaty Palms—The Neglected Art of Being Interviewed.* New York: Warner Business Books; 2005.

Reeves EG. *Can I Wear My Nose Ring to the Interview?* New York: Workman Publishing; 2009.

Yates M. *Knock 'em Dead 2017: The Ultimate Job Seekers Guide.* Avon, MA: Adams Media; 2016.

Networking

Baber A, Waymon L. *Make Your Contacts Count.* 2nd ed. New York: AMACOM; 2007.

Baker WE. *Networking Smart.* Lincoln, NE: iUIniverse.com; 2000.

Bjorseth LD. *Breakthrough Networking.* 3rd ed. Lisle, IL: Duoforce Enterprises; 2009.

Pierson O. *Highly Effective Networking.* Franklin Lakes, NJ: Career Press; 2009.

Robinett J. *How to Be a Power Connector: the 5+50+100 Rule for Turning Your Business Network into Profits.* New York: McGraw-Hill Education; 2014.

Zack D. *Networking for People Who Hate Networking: A Field Guide for Introverts, the Overwhelmed, and the Underconnected.* San Francisco: Berrett-Koehler Publishers; 2010.

Preparing Correspondence

Beatty RH. *The Perfect Cover Letter.* 3rd ed. New York: John Wiley and Sons; 2003.

Beatty RH. *175 High-Impact Cover Letters.* 3rd ed. New York: John Wiley and Sons; 2002.

Innes J. *The Cover Letter Book: Your Definitive Guide to Writing the Perfect Cover Letter.* 2nd ed. Upper Saddle River: FT Press; 2012.

Kennedy JL. *Cover Letters for Dummies.* 3rd ed. Indianapolis, IN: Wiley Publishing; 2009.

Noble DF. *Gallery of Best Cover Letters.* 4th ed. Indianapolis, IN: JIST Works; 2012.

Podesta S, Paxton A. *201 Killer Cover Letters.* 3rd ed. Washington, DC: McGraw-Hill Companies; 2014.

Yates M. *Cover Letters That Knock 'em Dead.* 11th ed. Avon, MA: Adams Media Corporation; 2014.

Preparing Personal Career Statements

Richardson J. *Mastering the Personal Statement.* Toronto: Richardson Press; 2000.

Stelzer RJ. *How to Write a Winning Personal Statement for Graduate and Professional School.* 3rd ed. Lawrenceville, NJ: Thomson Peterson's; 2002.

Stewart MA. *Perfect Personal Statement.* 4th ed. Lawrenceville, NJ: Thomson Peterson's; 2009.

Preparing Portfolios

Campbell DM, Cignetti PB, Melenyzer BJ, Nettles DH, Wyman RM. *How to Develop a Professional Portfolio: A Manual for Teachers.* 6th ed. New York: Pearson Education; 2013.

Costantino PM, DeLorenzo MN. *Developing a Professional Teaching Portfolio—A Guide to Success.* 3rd ed. Boston: Allyn and Bacon; 2008.

Heath M. *Electronic Portfolios: A Guide to Professional Development and Assessment.* Worthington, OH: Lindworth Publishing; 2004.

Seldin P. *The Teaching Portfolio—A Practical Guide to Improved Performance and Promotion/Tenure Decisions.* 4th ed. Boston: Anker Publishing Company; 2010.

Williams AG, Hall KA. *Creating Your Career Portfolio: At-a-Glance Guide for Students.* 3rd ed. Upper Saddle River: Prentice Hall; 2005.

Professional Image

Bixler S, Nix-Rice N. *The New Professional Image: Dress Your Best for Every Business Situation.* 2nd ed. Avon, MA: F+W Publication Company; 2005.

Caspersson DM. *Power Etiquette—What You Don't Know Can Kill Your Career.* Washington, DC: American Management Association International; 2009.

Hammer DP, Berger BA, Beardsley RS, Easton MR. Student professionalism. *Am J Pharm Educ.* 2003:67(3):Article 96.

Kelly WN, Sogol EM. *The Good Pharmacist—Characteristics, Virtues, and Habits.* Oldsmar, FL: William N. Kelly Consulting; 2011.

Post P. *Essential Manners for Men: What to Do, When to Do It, and Why.* 2nd ed. New York: Harper-Collins Publishers; 2012.

Ramsey L. *Manners That Sell—Adding the Polish That Builds Profits.* Gretna, LA: Pelican Press; 2008.

Social Media

Awl D. *Facebook Me!* 2nd ed. Berekeley: Peachpit Press; 2010.

McFedries P. *Twitter – Tips, Tricks and Tweets.* Indianapolis, IN: Wiley Publishing; 2010.

Morris T. *All a Twitter.* Indianapolis, IN: Pearson Education; 2009.

Safko L, Brake DK. *The Social Media Bible.* 3rd ed. Hoboken: John Wiley and Sons; 2012.

Vermeiren J. *How to Really Use LinkedIn.* 2nd ed. North Charleston, SC: BookSurge; 2011.

General Reference

Garneer BA. *Garner's Modern American Usage.* 3rd ed. New York: Oxford University Press; 2009.

Publication Manual of the American Psychological Association. 6th ed. Washington, DC: American Psychological Association; 2009.

Sabin WA. *The Gregg Reference Manual.* 11th ed. New York: The McGraw-Hill Companies; 2010.

Strunk W, White EB. *The Elements of Style.* 4th ed. Needham Heights, MA: Allyn and Bacon; 2009.

Style Manual: An official guide to the form and style of Federal Government printing. 30th ed. Washington, DC: United States Government Printing Office; 2008.

The Chicago Manual of Style. 16th ed. Chicago: The University of Chicago Press; 2010.

Index